The Eagle and the Serpent

A Bi-Literacy Autobiography

Ignacio G. Palacios

Hamilton Books
A member of
The Rowman & Littlefield Publishing Group
Lanham • Boulder • New York • Toronto • Plymouth, UK

Copyright © 2007 by
Hamilton Books
4501 Forbes Boulevard
Suite 200
Lanham, Maryland 20706
Hamilton Books Acquisitions Department (301) 459-3366

Estover Road
Plymouth PL6 7PY
United Kingdom

All rights reserved
Printed in the United States of America
British Library Cataloging in Publication Information Available

Library of Congress Control Number: 2007932647
ISBN-13: 978-0-7618-3831-9 (paperback : alk. paper)
ISBN-10: 0-7618-3831-7 (paperback : alk. paper)

∞™ The paper used in this publication meets the minimum
requirements of American National Standard for Information
Sciences—Permanence of Paper for Printed Library Materials,
ANSI Z39.48—1992

I want to dedicate this book to my wife Cynthia, and my sons Andrew and John-Mark, for without them my life would not be what it is today, rich and blessed because of each one of them.

Contents

Foreword — vii
Acknowledgments — ix
Introduction — xi

1. The Imperfect Seven — 1
2. Scholars' Views — 5
3. Childhood in Mexico — 9
4. Just What is Literacy? — 17
5. Immigration to the US — 21
6. Acculturation in America — 29
7. Metamorphosis — 47
8. Current Literacies — 53
9. The View From Here — 59

Appendix: Immigrant Children at Ellis' Door — 67
Works Consulted and Cited — 73
About the Author — 75

Foreword

Ignacio Palacios in this volume follows in the footsteps of Mexican –American writers such as Richard Rodriquez and Tomás Mario Kalmar by reflecting on his experiences with literacy in two languages, Spanish and English. Unlike Rodriquez, however, Palacios' journey brings him to embrace bilingualism and biliteracy. His migration as a generation 1.5 child from Monterrey through Chicago and back to Aztlan, brings him to see the eagle and the serpent as his unifying metaphor.

Palacios' transformation or metamorphosis, as he calls it, comes primarily through family, education, and religion which allow him to exercise his bilingual bilteracy. More than a contribution to the now-established genre of immigrant autobiography, this work presents socially-situated episodes that enable the author to reflect on the struggles to preserve one language and emerge in another. Like the childish narrative voice in Sandra Cisneros' stories, Ignacio's voice invites us to see and hear his world. His way with words and deeds and things, expressed in the multiple genres of narrative, exposition, and poetry, allows the reader to understand the coming into being of his identity, the struggle through rejection, to community, a life among multiple cultures, literacies, and people.

Professor Dan J. Tannacito
Indiana University of Pennsylvania
Indiana, PA 15705
January 28, 2007

Acknowledgments

I am grateful to God for guiding me in writing and finishing this autobiographical account, and to my wife Cynthia for helping to review it.

I am grateful to the publishers and editors at University Press of America for guiding me in the final typesetting guidelines and final publication of this volume.

My professors at Indiana University of Pennsylvania inspired me through their course work; in the many tasks involved in their courses, I was giving birth to the ideas in this volume.

I am especially grateful to Dr. Dan Tannacito, for it was in his class on second language literacy that the real manuscript was born, in short essay format.

I quoted some of my autobiographical material from pages 55-60 from my own dissertation: Palacios, Ignacio, 2001. *An ESL/Literacy Center: a qualitative study of perspectives and practices of immigrant adults and literacy facilitators*. Unpublished Doctoral Dissertation, Indiana University of Pennsylvania.

I am grateful for friends who have believed in this project and have shown their support.

Introduction

At the outset I must make clear that I am an American; my political loyalty is to my beloved adopted country, The United States of America. This book entails the process of my change from a Mexican child of immigrant parents to an adult American citizen. It's a process that has involved cultural, linguistic and religious changes.

In this volume, I have related some experiences in my life, both in Spanish and in English literacy development. It is an illustration of the bilingual/bicultural experience of acculturation and assimilation: a process of change, both culturally and linguistically. I do this in three levels: autobiographical experiences in bi-literacy acquisition, reflections from the viewpoint of a bilingual/bicultural Mexican-American adult, and finally, an analysis of the process evident in my experience. Interspersed in the autobiographical experiences, I reflect on my current perspectives on what happened in the past, and I intersperse poems, which are an expression of my feelings at this point in time about the experiences I went through in the past. I also reflect upon my spiritual journey of religious conversion, from Mexican Catholicism to American Evangelicalism.

I am a first generation Mexican-American, undergoing linguistic, cultural, and religious change. As a child of Mexican immigrants, I grew up as a generation 1.5 individual in the United States. Though I have undergone anomie, acculturation, and emotional and cultural struggles in this process, English has become my second, yet dominant language, and American culture has shaped my way of being. Still, because of my cultural background in early childhood, I consider myself a Mexican-American, not forsaking my native Spanish language and culture. I am now an American, having become one like many other immigrants. Now, I am currently a TESOL, English, and

Spanish college professor. At this stage, I believe I have learned to live with the process of acculturation. Immigration for any people means inevitable change—a process of discovery and challenge—if the immigrant learns to adjust, accept, and hope.

Four caveats are in order here. First, in my dissertation (Palacios, 2001), though not dealing with my autobiography per se, I have already rather briefly sketched some of my own autobiographical material. In this present book, I have greatly expanded, revised and updated a lot of that material. Thus, at times I do quote my dissertation in several places, especially from pages 55-60 in my dissertation which are autobiographical in nature. Second, most names have been changed or remain pseudonyms to protect any person's interests. Third, the facts and events related are my own recollections; thus, I am responsible for any errors, lapses of memory, or omissions. Fourth, I use figurative language, symbols and figures to illustrate the metaphor of my life: a metamorphosis, a cross-cultural transformation from the early years to adult life. These metaphors, symbols and figures are not meant to be offensive to any sensibilities, but only meant as literary devices to illustrate my points.

Chapter One

The Imperfect Seven

El Aguila y la Serpiente sobre un nopal se treparon...
The Eagle and the Serpent atop a cactus they climbed...

I have just tried all keyboard types and fonts and I am frustrated! My computer refuses to type the number seven crossed! I miss my number seven crossed. Have I been robbed of it entirely? I'll have to resort to an empty space between parentheses to show the imperfectness of seven ( ). I guess my early literacy is useless in today's information/computer world. For the story of the missing crossed seven, I'll have to say it all started back when....

In Texas, my fifth grade teacher emphatically told me not to write the number 7 crossed since it could be confused with an F. My childhood mind asked: "What? Say that again?" I couldn't understand how the number seven crossed ( ) could be confused by any sensible person with an F. To me, an F and a 7 were as distinct as black and white.

Now, in Mexico my first grade teacher had carefully taught us the concept of seven and the written symbol for 7.

"Es como un bastoncito con un palito que lo cruza," she showed us on the blackboard. So with my child fingers, meticulously, painstakingly, I endeavored to draw the little cane with a stick across it. After a few more tries, my little fingers could finally, crudely, draw a little cane with a stick across it — the number seven ( ). Now after several more of my attempts, the teacher told us to write a whole page of the number seven in our tablets for homework, as was the common practice.

The next day, after I had laboriously written the number seven about one hundred times, the teacher was not satisfied since I had not left spacing between numbers. How was I to know that any little canes needed spaces between them? The literacy practice unknown to me was that any little canes

Figure 1.1. Eagle and flags

crossed needed room to themselves, personal room to grow, I suppose! In fact, all the pages of numbers and letters we had to write taught me that all letters and numbers needed personal space. Nonetheless, I finally learned to make the beautiful little cane crossed. And the next year, I would be seven in the second grade!

THE PURPOSE IN THIS AUTOBIOGRAPHY

I will return to the imperfect seven story later, but first I will relate some experiences in my life, both in Spanish and in English literacy, which speak to me of the bilingual/bicultural experience: a process of change, both culturally and linguistically. I will attempt to do this in three levels: autobiographical narratives in bi-literacy acquisition, reflections from the viewpoint of a bilingual/bicultural Mexican-American adult, and finally, some scholarly analysis of the process evident in my experience. I do this in ten major sections:

The Imperfect Seven
Scholars' Views
Childhood in Mexico
Just What is Literacy?
Immigration to US
Acculturation in America
Metamorphosis
Current Literacies
The View From Here
Appendix: Immigrant Children at Ellis' Door.

Interspersed in the autobiographical narratives, I will reflect as a scholar on my current perspectives on what happened in the past, and I will intersperse several poems, which are an expression of my feelings at this point in time about the experiences I went through.

A pattern seems to emerge from my life: I am a first generation Mexican-American, undergoing linguistic, cultural, and religious change. I am that generation 1.5 individual who came to the United States as a child of 10, going on 11, with my Mexican immigrant parents. Though I have undergone anomie, acculturation, and emotional and cultural struggles in this process of change, English has become my second language and American culture has shaped my way of being. I have become an American. Still, I consider myself a Mexican-American, not forsaking my native Spanish language and culture. At this stage, I believe I have learned to live with the process of change and acculturation. Immigration for any person means change, inevitable change. But change can be a process of discovery and challenge, if the immigrant learns to adjust, accept, and hope.

Chapter Two

Scholars' Views

At the 2006 TESOL Convention in Tampa, Florida, I was privileged to sit in a session dealing with generation 1.5 students (first generation children of immigrant families who become educated in the United States). It was a team presentation. One particular presenter was giving characteristics of these students as most likely to fail in school and even drop out of the "literacy" and acculturation system in the US. When I asked, "What about the person who succeeds and becomes bilingual and bi-literate, to the point of obtaining a doctorate in English?" The speaker answered that such a person would not be of much interest to his own "research" agenda. I replied, "I am that generation 1.5 individual who has succeeded and obtained a Ph.D. in English!" The presenter ignored my comment, while another attendee commented to me that she also knew of some other generation 1.5 people who had actually succeeded, but agreed with me that people like us are often ignored in favor of the stereotypical ignorant failed immigrants!

Lutz agrees with me that success in acquisition of L2 and C2 and maintenance of L1 and C1 has not been validated: "A great deal of research and attention has focused on the academic problems facing students with limited English proficiency, such as low levels of achievement, placement into lower grade levels or educational tracks, and high dropout levels" (2004, p. 2).

Though the one doing research on generation 1.5 people would say I am not of interest, I disagree and hope my own bilingual bi-literacy autobiography shows one who has succeeded, not one who has failed as predicted by generation 1.5 researchers, prophets of failure. I propose that my narrative would give a different position than popular authors have given. For instance, a second generation Mexican-American, Richard Rodriguez (1982), has given in his excellent autobiography *Hunger of Memory* a negative view of bilingual or bi-literate education and of bilingual education proponents. He regrets his loss of his native language and culture, but says he gained his public language and culture, namely American culture and the English language. Rodriguez in his autobiographical account relates that by his own choice he decided to sever his private home language and embrace his public education discourse abilities. For Rodriguez, his gain of L2 (second language) and C2 (second culture), seemed to be a somewhat nostalgic though at times a pathetic process. Lea Ramsdell (2004) states:

> Rodriguez equates the loss of his mother tongue, Spanish, with the inevitable separation that all children who become educated experience as they develop a public persona removed from the private sphere. While he uses this assertion to support his argument against bilingual education, he does not hide the grief that he feels over the loss of intimacy that came about in his family as theirs became a primarily English-speaking household. Yet he refuses to consider the possibility that the two languages could have occupied both the private and public spheres. For Rodriguez, Spanish and English exist at opposite poles; to retain allegiance to Spanish means to seal one's future as a member of the working class, whereas mastering English is the entry ticket into the gringo world of economic success. (p. 3)

Though I have become bilingual and bi-literate myself, I do not think I have endured the same process of alienation and rejection of my first language and culture. I am still a bilingual and bicultural individual. In fact, I have obtained my Ph.D. in English, my second and dominant language, and have become an English teacher and a TESOL teacher-trainer for both American and international students. I also have been teaching ESL to non-native speakers, those who, like me years ago, are presently undergoing a process of learning English as a second language. Additionally, I am a college teacher of Spanish, my first language, which I have maintained. I believe since I was already literate in Spanish, my L1, I was able to transfer literacy skills into my L2, English, early in my educational experience in the United States. In fact, Lutz' (2004) research on biliterate individuals concludes that "biliterate students are significantly more likely to complete high school compared to their monolingual peers," and "biliterate students are also significantly more likely to enter college, and particularly, a bachelor's degree program, than are their peers who speak only English" (p. 7). In this biliteracy autobiography I hope to validate the maintenance of L1 and C1, as well as the embrace of an L2 and C2, as additional literacies, or additive bilingualism. Lea Ramsdell (2004) believes that linguistic autobiographies are attempts to define one's self. She claims that autobiographies appeal especially to bilinguals because they tell their development of L1 and L2 in which they define themselves (p. 2). The act of writing our stories shapes our identity.

Gloria Anzaldúa (1987), on the opposite pole to Rodriguez (1982), embraces her bilingualism and glories in her multiple literacies, including Tex-Mex, Spanglish. Ramsdell (2004) quotes Anzaldúa asserting that her language is her own identity:

> So if you want to really hurt me, talk badly about my language. Ethnic identity is twin skin to linguistic identity — I am my language. Until I can accept as legitimate Chicano Texas Spanish, Tex-Mex and all the other languages I speak, I cannot accept the legitimacy of myself.... (p.5)

Thus, I have chosen my title from a poem I wrote: *The Eagle and the Serpent* (poem included in a later chapter), which symbolizes the commingled and coexisting nature of bilingualism and biculturalism. These two symbols, though at times in conflict, are together one and the same emblem. They represent who I am.

Here's the rest of my story.

Chapter Three

Childhood in Mexico

CUENTOS DE GÜELITA Y MADRINA: AN EARLY ORAL WORLD

As I was endeavoring to write my autobiography, I came across Ron Padgett's book *Creative Reading* (1997), in which he offers an outline questionnaire for creating a literacy narrative. His questionnaire helped me to focus my ideas on early childhood experiences. Nevertheless, though I am not being critical of Padgett's (1997, ch. 3) questionnaire for a personal literacy story, I realize his questionnaire is somewhat idealistic. Though his questions may be good for a general first language literacy autobiography, I believe his questions would most likely refer to an American middle-class person acquiring a native language growing up in the mid-twentieth century in suburbia. I think he must be assuming a *before* kindergarten/first grade reading/writing knowledge or acquaintance.

However, as I reflected upon this, I have come to realize that before school, mine was an oral world! My favorite memories are of the evenings in Monterrey, Mexico, when my paternal grandmother would tell us children *cuentos* (stories)—in Spanish, of course! Late in the evening, under the moonlight, and sitting on the front doorstep of her two-room *vecindad* apartment, I would become absorbed in her magical world of words. Güelita (short for Abuelita, affectionate term for grandmother) would tell the story of the sun and its love-affair with the moon. The sun was jealous and would hide his wife during the day, for fear of would-be suitors. When one suitor tried to enamour the moon, the sun would avenge itself by changing people into bedposts overnight! Then there was the traditional lore, "La llorona" (a mother's ghost who goes about bewailing the fact that she has murdered her children, ¡Ay mis hijos!), "La mano pachona" (a hairy hand coming out of nowhere, that would grab you and try to kill you), "El cuco" (the bogeyman that would get you if you didn't go to sleep! How was I going to sleep after that?). Güelita's fairytales weren't the canon of American or European fairy tales!

My great aunt, on my mother's side, whom all the family called Madrina Linda, would instruct us in our Catholic traditions, teaching me my prayers and the rosary litanies. I remember at Christmas time she would set up a *nacimiento*, an elaborate manger scene, the village of Bethlehem filled with little clay statues of people for each of whom she had their own individual story to tell. For instance, Bartolo was always lying down instead of chopping wood because he was too slothful. Even when the other people in the village standing around him told him to get up to go worship the newborn child Jesus, he would rather sleep than worship! The Three Kings were coming as they traditionally did, on a horse, a camel and an elephant. Because they didn't have enough room on their riding animals, they also had to have a little caravan of donkeys and mules for all their luggage!

Now the shepherds had to prepare their feast for this most meaningful event, so they would roast their sheep over little fires (represented by red lights under ceramic kindle wood). While the sheep was roasting, the *tortillera* (tortilla-maker woman) was busy making tortillas by hand and placing them on the *comal* (open grill) over the open fire. To the side of the tortillas she had to have a few *chiles* roasting to go with the roast sheep, for no Mexican would want to have a feast without tortillas and *chiles*.

El *ermitaño*, the old monk-like hermit, with his long flowing white beard and dressed in a black monk's cowl, was always in the cave and had his rosary in his praying hands; he had to be in constant prayer, for the Devil himself, grinning menacingly, sat right on top of the cave trying to tempt him every minute. The old hermit's life was a miserable one indeed! I had noticed that the clay figurine of the red devil was part of the same clay as the top of the cave! Never could the *ermitaño* be rid of the Devil!

The beautiful waterfall cascading down the little hill was filled with clay figures of swans and ducks, and occasional fish, which were seen in the blue-white angel-hair (which represented water) covering the aluminum foil fountain. In the village itself, each little person was heading straight for the stable, each one bringing some gift to the soon-to-be-born-King. One woman would bring a duck, another a chicken; some man would bring a pig, another a turkey. The King Himself was not placed in the manger until His very birthday, December 24, when all Bethlehem would be in a fiesta! Mexican shepherds couldn't go visit such royalty without bringing some precious gift from their farms!

My great-aunt delighted me with such tales! To this day, I still set up our traditional Nacimiento every Christmas season in our home.

Güelita and Madrina had their own stories to tell, one, on the one hand, mischievously grotesque, the other, on the other hand, whimsically sublime!

LAS POSADAS

Our main fiestas were the annual *posadas*. During nine days before *Noche Buena*, December 24, small groups of *vecinos* would walk from one house to another carrying a small platform on which appeared Mary on a donkey, guided by Joseph, and protected by a guardian Angel, who followed behind them. Traditional Cantos de Pedir Posada were sung as the pilgrims arrived at each home.

> En el nombre del cielo,
> Os pido posada.
> Pues no puede andar,
> Mi esposa amada.

So went the wailing-like song which represented Joseph's plea for lodging for his pregnant wife.

> Váyanse de aquí,
> Porque si me enfado,
> ¡Os voy a palear!

That would be the nasty reply of the people denying the pilgrims any lodging.

> Mi nombre es José,
> Mi esposa es María,
> Es Reina del Cielo,
> Y Madre va a ser,
> Del Divino Verbo.

The pleas continued until finally, the home was opened with joyful singing:

> Entren Santos Peregrinos, Peregrinos,
> Aunque es pobre la posada, la posada.
> Os la doy de corazón.

The people would join those inside who were prepared for the piñata and the following *tamalada*, the traditional Christmastime dinners, consisting mainly of tamales.

At Madrina's house, on December 24th, the family and neighbors would gather for our Noche Buena Rosary, La Acostada del Niño (the laying of the Babe) on the manger. Kneeling in front of the elaborate Nacimiento, all of us would repeat the litanies of the rosary.

> Dios te salve, María,
> Llena eres de gracia,
> El Señor es contigo.
> Bendita tú entre las mujeres,
> Y bendito el fruto de tu vientre, Jesús.

Once I had asked Madrina, "Por qué rezamos diez Ave Marías y solo un Padrenuestro?"

"The Virgin Mary is suffering because Jesus is to be born. So we have pity on her and concentrate our prayers on her, rather than on the Father."

I didn't understand anything about women giving birth, or why Mary had to suffer since she was already in Heaven, or so I had been taught.

Santa María, Madre de Dios . . . we faithfully continued with our litany. As two people knelt right in front of the Nacimiento facing each other, they held a plate filled with traditional *colaciones* (sugar confetti candy). Nestled in the center of the plate of colaciones was placed the Niño Dios, the Child God. Worshipers approached shuffling on their knees to kiss the statue's feet, while we sang

> Llega, llega, pecador,
> Llega, llega de rodillas,
> A adorar al Salvador,
> A Dios, Hijo de María.

Each of us would kiss the feet of the Niño, then take a candy into our mouths, as if doing communion.

Outside, preparing for the traditional cena de Noche Buena, the men drank their beers and swore fiercely as they laughed and joked about the ritual, creating their own parody of prayers. Inside we prayed to Mary,

> Ruega por nosotros (Pray for us).

The men were mocking with

> Ruega por los cacahuates (Pray for the peanuts).

Mamá Grande, my great grandmother, would come on her knees and kiss the Babe, but to my amazement would not take a candy, the promised favor for kissing the Child God. How holy my great-grandmother must be, kissing Him and taking nothing in return!

As we blew out the colorful candles, the smell of smoke filled the tiny room, and we got ready for the piñata and the traditional tamales.

LA RADIO Y LA TELE

I didn't have any books at home before school. I didn't go to nursery school or watch Sesame Street on TV, because we didn't own one before I went to school (besides, Sesame Street didn't come into my life until sixth grade in the U.S!) I didn't listen to any children stories on the radio; I heard only my mom's *radionovelas*, songs and news. Mother loved to listen to her *radionovelas* on the radio, for only the rich had televisions. *El Ojo de Vidrio* was a popular *radionovela* about a fabled supposed outlaw in Monterrey who had to hide in caves in the Cerro de la Silla (Saddle Mountain). He wore a glass eye, *el ojo de vidrio*, for which he was easily recognizable. He was often embroiled in trying to vindicate his innocence against cases in which he was being framed. One day, when I was five or six, the programs and the singing on the radio were interrupted, and I noticed all the adults looked extremely disturbed. I approached the table and drew near to the small green radio as I heard the news that Kennedy had been shot.

Later, though, at about age seven or eight, after I had already been in school, my family did get our first television set, so we would watch the Sunday night *Cuentos*, traditional fairy tales like Snow White and Cinderella. But before that, no one even thought about teaching me to read or write, though my Dad did teach me to tell time. There were no libraries I could go to in order to delve into the world of books; no one gave me books as a gift, except for my devotional at my first communion, but that happened after I was already in school. I did not have a book world before school.

Yet I didn't feel deprived, for mine was an oral world — my grandmother's and great-aunt's storytelling and religious instruction filled the void of books.

MY FIRST DISILLUSION — NOT A HAPPY COMMUNION!

"Los sacramentos de la ley de Dios son siete:

primero, bautismo,
segundo, confirmación.
tercero, eucarestía,
cuarto, extrema unción.

quinto, penitencia,
sexto, orden sacerdotal,
y séptimo matrimonio."

I recited my catechism litanies, as I stood swaying from side to side; the catechist glared down her nose and asked me to stand still while I recited the catechism doctrines in preparation for my First Communion, a Catholic rite of passage.

On Saturday five or six of us catechumens walked to the Iglesia de Guadalupe to meet with the priest and have our first confessional.

"Le he hecho cosas malas a mi hermano." I nervously told the priest.

"¿Qué cosas?" He wanted details.

Alarmed, I faltered "I have hit him and swore at him," hoping this would satisfy his nosiness. What other sibling naughtiness could I confess?

"All right. Now repeat the Credo after me."

As the priest recited the Creed, I followed his words, mumbling them back.

"Now go to the altar and kneel there and pray twenty Ave Marías, so God can forgive you, and you are absolved."

I knelt fearfully at the altar, the closest I had ever been to the Sacrament, behind the mysterious case, which I had been told contained the very Body and Blood of Christ.

"Dios te salve, María…" I prayed twenty times.

Once all the boys had gone through the confessions and the penitential prayers at the altar, the priest dismissed us and told us we could go play out in the church back yard. The boys headed out and began a game of soccer.

My first disillusionment came when I heard one of the boys yelling at another companion: "#@%$^, #@%$^, ¡no seas #%$@&^!"

The other boy had done something he didn't like, so he was swearing at him.

Having just come out of the church and having just said our confessions, and having been before the holy altar, right before Christ's precious Body and Blood, I was appalled at the boy's language. I took my faith seriously, but I realized boys were not holy creatures, in spite of confessions and prayers. Was that a real repentance, if we were to go on sinning minutes later, and right before First Communion? I went the next day disillusioned and took the host in my mouth, hoping I had not sinned to be struck down and die for taking the host unworthily.

¿PADRECITO NACHITO?

Mother was hoping I'd become a *Monaguillo*, an acolyte or altar boy, or maybe even a *Padrecito*, a priest, since I seemed to take faith seriously. Madrina had been my primary teacher in the things of Christ through her stories around the Nacimiento.

The neighborhood *estanquillo* half a block away sold ice slushies, popcorn, *tostaditas con frijoles y queso*, and rented out comic books. I ordered a *tostadita roja* with beans and cheese, sprinkled with *Salsa Búfalo*, and out of the corner of my eye I noticed hanging on the short clothes line (on which were comics held up with clothes pins), a copy of an illustrated story of *Jesucristo*. I wanted to rent it out, but was too embarrassed to ask for it, fearing being made fun of by my amigos, so I asked my mother to rent it for me. She took me to the *estanquillo* and told the woman what I wanted. They allowed me to rent out the illustrated story. I loved learning about the life of Jesus. My mother was sure I'd turn out to be a priest yet!

After reading the story and later watching the movie about *La vida y pasión de Jesucristo* during Semana Santa (Holy Week) on my aunt's television set, I decided I wanted to build myself a cross so I could carry it like Jesus did. One of my aunts saw me positioning the cross against a wall, while I leaned back onto it, holding my arms out as if crucified. My aunt was shocked as I lay my head back and rolled my eyes, as if I had just died. Mother told her, "Nachito va a ser padrecito." But I really wanted to be a teacher, not a priest!

We moved from that vecindad to another vecindad. I walked to the other apartment carrying my home-made cross. I didn't care that others looked at me kind of strangely. I thought maybe I'd become a monk!

Through my grandmother's storytelling, my great aunt's religious instruction, and my parents influences, my early years were really an oral world, but it was in school that I was introduced to the world of reading and writing.

MY SPANISH LITERACY

In first grade, I remember learning cursive writing. To get us ready for cursive writing, our teacher had us practice hand motor coordination through *ovalo* and *lluvia*. Señorita Virginia, our young teacher, the respected authority figure, would have us fill pages full of spirals (ovalo) and closely knit zigzags (lluvia), which I painstakingly tried to do as neatly as I could, but Señorita Virginia was not pleased because mine did not look like hers - - mine were too sloppy!

Then, she had us buy our texts printed in cursive writing, and we were expected to learn to read and write in cursive. Not until second grade did the government provide our books free. One of my first lessons was about Mamá. I remember it well:

Mamá, mamá,
Mi mamá me mima.

Amo a mi mamá!
(Translation: Mama, Mama, My Mama pampers me. I love my Mama).

Not only did we learn to read, we had to memorize the lesson, recite it by memory back to the teacher, and copy it in our tablets in cursive writing. That was learning to read and write for us!

My school experiences, however, seemed different for me from my literacy experiences at home. When I was a boy, *mi Papá* was involved in public performances in theater, and on the radio in Monterrey, Mexico. Though his dad, Güelito, had pulled him out of school in fifth grade because of economic necessity, *mi Papá* loved learning, and he became a self-taught man. He was an amateur actor in plays. Often in our two room apartment, I would hear him memorize and recite his lines out loud. I admired his abilities and would watch with wonder as he performed in plays and sang songs in theatres and on the radio. He recorded a single personal copy or a 78 rpm record (not for commercial resale), with his favorite song ("Adios mi chaparrita," by Mexican author Ignacio Fernández Esperón, 1930s). Father, in 1967, left my family in Mexico as he immigrated to the United States. Mother, of course, like the rest of us was saddened by his departure. My Dad's song was reminiscent of his departure and hopeful return. Here's the gist of the first stanza of father singing this song: Good-bye my dear one, don't cry for me; if I leave, I'll come back soon.

As a result, I was learning songs, stories, and dramas right at home in Spanish. Sometimes I would take a peek at Dad's play scripts as he rehearsed them, and I was amazed and proud to think my Father was an actor. When I was about eight or nine, he even had me be in a stage production in one of the modern impressionist theater pieces, *Disonancias*, at the Teatro Municipal de Monterrey, in which I played a small non-speaking role as a page. To this day, my parents have a copy of the newspaper article with our picture of all of us as actors in the play. As a singer, my father was always learning new songs and singing them at home, in theaters in Monterrey, and on the radio; and as a poetry orator, he was always reciting verses and occasionally teaching me a few, though I don't remember any except a title, *El Brindis del Bohemio*, a famous Spanish poem. Father was literate. He was a thinker. He was involved in a socialist political party and was a union activist at the Fundidora de Monterrey, northern México's then famous steel plant. My father was a critical thinker. Did he have school literacy? He had a sixth grade education. Is school literacy necessary to become a critical thinker, actor, activist, and leader?

Chapter Four

Just What is Literacy?

Literacy is most probably related to a culture's view of what makes a person function as a successful and productive member of that culture, usually entailing some sort of communicative and sociolinguistic competence, whether using oral and/or visual arbitrary and conventional symbols. It is related to a knowledge of symbols or meaning; thus it has a semiotic mysticism, an almost powerfully magical dimension. There may be different types of literacies, depending on the culture's view. Some authors such as Gee (1991) describe discourse literacies—primary discourses, secondary discourses, powerful literacies, etc.—meanwhile, Baynham (1995) describes critical literacy, while Street (1984) discusses ideological literacies, etc. For instance, in many western academic settings, literacy may be seen as a critical competence in reading-writing and understanding-speaking of academic discourses/languages. However, in the mountain village of San Ildefonso, in northern Mexico (which I have visited as an adult missionary in Mexico), there is no such thing as a university; here literacy may simply be seen by these mountain people as an articulateness and facility of language, especially in public speaking or church sermons, including an ability to read and interpret Bible texts, and an ability for what some US academics may term "rudimentary survival writing" skills, or plain "functional, useless," literacy. Yet it is not useless for their own purposes (after all, who decides who is literate or not?).

On the other hand, for a family friend in Arkansas, whom I'll call Linda, literacy is the oral ability to communicate thoughts, to dictate messages through her voice activated computer, and the ability to read books or computer texts, and/or be read to and understand these "oral" and visual readings. Linda is a handicapped twenty-something year old young woman (born without her four limbs). Of course she must rely on orality/vision because of her handicap. Blind people rely on the tactile modality for reading Braille. Nonetheless, these people would still have critical thinking skills, and would be conversant in their types of literacies—as needed in their contexts. What would be considered literacy for a child such as Helen Keller? She became famous because she actually did become "literate" through knowledge of the world first, then knowledge of literate discourses (reading/ writing).

During my ethnographic research for my dissertation dealing with second language literacy, I researched what constituted literacy in an ESL/Literacy center for immigrant adults. Through my qualitative dissertation, which involved observations, interviews, and analysis, I discovered that there are multiple perspectives and practices associated with literacy. In fact, I concluded the following in my own work: "Implicit and explicit literacy perspectives at [the] learning center shape processes of literacy events because... established discourses from L1 and L2 promote certain types of literacy practices. These in turn are a mere reflection of perspectives" (Palacios, 2001, p. 6). I believe literacy is defined based on practices in contexts.

For these reasons, literacy may be understood as a situated, sociolinguistic, psychological, communicative competence which may or may not include the physical ability to "write" with hands, but which most probably includes an ability to read (and read between the lines, or read the world, to use a Freirian term), to read print with eyes and/or hands (as for Braille) or without hands only eyes (as for Linda) and ears, and which fits the needs/wants of the communicants. Now Linda, or the San Ildefonso church person, (or even Helen Keller in her blind, deaf and dumb state, without verbal/visual communication with the outside world) are not dummies just because they may not fulfill Gee's or Baynham's or Street's elaborate and complex definitions of literacy.

Nonetheless, if a member from the San Ildefonso church community decided to move to Saltillo, Coahuila, Mexico, the capital city of the state near the village, he/she would most likely need to learn or acquire further critical psycho/sociolinguistic competencies in an urban literacy environment, thus expanding his/her types of literacies or adding more literacies. The person would be multi-literate! If Linda ever wanted to become a college professor, more than likely, she would have to undergo rigorous academic/social training in "unknown" academic discourses to achieve her ambitious goal. At this point, she has graduated from high school and has taken some college computer courses and some Spanish courses. She's a Black native English speaker who wishes to someday become self-sufficient, caring for herself independent of her adoptive parents. Helen Keller would be an ideal example of a "literate" individual who had no recourse to visual/auditory modes, but had a critical psycho/sociolinguistic competence in interacting with "literate" communicants, through Braille, and tactile modes. None of these people are dummies, even if they don't measure up to the "scholars" definitions of literacy.

So what can I call literacy? I believe literacy is a semiotic understanding of discourse symbols, arbitrarily chosen by inter-communicants and having psycho/socially conventionalized agreed upon meanings for the literate ones. The initiated, the literate ones, have the power to foretell or predict what's coming, what's between the lines of oral/visual "text", to ordain their lives or prophesy what's coming in their lives or those of others. I don't want to define literacy in such a way as to exclude those who may not measure up to my yardstick, as I sense some scholars would despairingly, though innocently, do. But the literate ones know when they are literate. This magic is called literacy.

Ron Padgett, in his book about Creative Reading (1997), says that a "magic moment" "jelled" for him and he discovered that he could read (p. 7). Also, he says "All words have magical properties" (p. 58); reading backward "activates one's feeling for the magical nature of words" (p. 71); "juxtapositions" of words and pictures in newspapers "have an oracular power" (p. 79); So it's all about magic—the magic of literacy. It's more than print—it's the world.

So it was for Helen Keller when the magic moment came and she realized everything had a name!

BI-LITERACIES

What then would be a bi-literate individual? If literacy can be defined as I did above (a semiotic understanding of discourse symbols, arbitrarily chosen by inter-communicants and having psycho/socially conventionalized agreed upon meanings for the literate ones), then bi-literacy would include the capacity to have such a semiotic understanding of discourse symbols through more than one language, specifically two systems of communication. Therefore, I would have to say that a bilingual, bi-literate individual is multitalented for having such an ability! Rather than see a bilingual as "a-lingual" (having no language ability, neither in one or the other language) or even yet as "illiterate" (knowing neither as a literate person) as some have proposed, or even worse still deride bilingual/biliteracy language programs, one ought to laud such marvelous efforts of the human genius! I agree with Lutz (2004) who concludes from her own study that:

> Although Latino students face barriers to educational attainment compared to the majority group, the relative success of bi-literate students, compared to those who speak only English, does not support the hypothesis suggested by the

assimilation perspective, which would predict that "only English" offers the greatest educational advantage. Instead, in terms of educational attainment, the ability to read and write in both English and Spanish appears to offer bi-literate students a significant advantage over their peers who are proficient only in English. (p. 7)

Some people may ask, "But what about the students who apparently learn neither language well? How do you account for them?" Richard Rodriguez (1983) would probably be in favor of teaching them English only. But if I am of any example, I learned my early oral literacy skills in my native language first; then, at school I learned my reading/writing skills in that language which I already knew. When my family immigrated to the United States, I was ten going on eleven. I was able to transfer Spanish literacy skills successfully from my first language into my second language, English. Why not allow bilingual students to have such a chance? Why not allow the home language to be taught first, including literacy skills? Then additive bilingualism can become a resource, as English is added as another vehicle for oral and written communication. I went on to obtain my Ph.D. in English, though it's my second language; yet I have maintained my first language and use it on a regular basis in all skills: listening, speaking, reading, writing—even at an advanced graduate level!

Having mused on this topic, now I will return to my own bi-literacy learning process.

Chapter Five

Immigration to the US

MY FAMILY'S EMIGRATION FROM MEXICO

My parents made a conscious choice to come to the United States when I was ten. My father already had been living in the Chicago area for a year or two before he obtained papers for his entire family to join him.

"Papi tiene carro. ¡Tenemos carro!" I ran outside overjoyed to see it was true that Father had come back from the States and brought with him an old white 1960s Ford Falcon station wagon, with which he planned to take us all to the US.

"Nos vamos a los Estados Unidos," was the fateful news.

"No quiero dejar a Nane (maternal grandmother)," I cried. My maternal grandmother was my dearest second mother. We affectionately started calling her Nane. I was the first born son and grandson. It is said that when I was learning to talk I couldn't say Mamá Grande, so I would say, "Ma Nane." The appellative stuck and all cousins, aunts, uncles, and even neighbors called her Nane.

"We'll just go for a few years and make money, and come back to Mexico," my father assured us.

"How many years?" We children begged to know.

"Unos cinco años," my father answered.

"Will we have a house with a yard with grass like Tía Ninfa's?" I dreamed of a real home, as I pictured homes in the United States.

"Yes," was my father's promise, which he never could keep in the US. Father had thought of taking us to Chicago, where he had just spent a year working, and had previously obtained his worker's papers and permission to immigrate his entire family.

However, we did not go straight to Chicago; instead, we lived for a few months in a small rural area in Southern Texas. "At that time, my brother, my sister and I felt devastated, because we had come from a large metropolis, Monterrey. In the rural area of Brownsville, Texas, we felt like we had been put back in time!" (Palacios, 2001, p. 55). In Mexico I remembered visiting elderly distant relatives (aunts of my mother's cousins) back in the *ranchos*, but rural Texas did not remind us at all of the pleasant memories with relatives in Mexico. "Our perfect world had turned imperfect! Whereas in Mexico we were becoming middle class well-educated "literate" people, in the U. S. we were thought of as poor ignorant Mexicans - - fitting the 'illiterate' stereotype of Mexican- Americans in the Southwest!" (Palacios, 2001, p.55).

In Chicago Heights, I remember in eighth grade English literature we were reading a short story about a wet-back who comes to the US just to earn some meager income. I recall my classmate asking me, "Did you use to ride a donkey when you lived in Mexico?" I was appalled! "No, I come from a big city, Monterrey, known as the little Chicago. I've never even seen a donkey!" Of course I had seen donkeys, but I had not been from the *ranchos*, a *ranchero*, so why would such a dumb question be asked? I was a city person! Why must all Mexican immigrants have the stereotype of wearing white pants and shirts made of *manta*, of wearing a big sombrero, and sleeping under a cactus?

I came from a city; I had been in a drama on stage in a big city; I had learned to recite my litanies; I had become literate in Spanish in Mexico. I was not an illiterate *campesino*! Why couldn't my previous literacy skills be validated in this new country?

REFLECTIONS ON CULTURAL CHANGE

For this section I am relying on my dissertation (Palacios, 2001) to repeat some words and ideas relevant to this autobiography:

> Zentella (1997) says: "The model that children of ethnolinguistic minorities reproduce is subject to the 'symbolic domination' (Bordieu, 1991) of the dominant class of monolingual English speakers, that is, to that class's [sic] definition of legitimate and illegitimate language and culture" (p. 2). Perhaps this symbolic domination was also evident in the cultural/social relationships we were experiencing as new immigrants, though as children all we could sense is that we didn't belong, and perhaps the environment is what produced the greatest culture shock.
>
> My brother (six), my sister (eight) and I (ten) thought the United States was ugly, perhaps in more ways than one, and we wanted to go back to our modern Mexican city! Not only was the rural country chaparral environment dry and

ugly, but people didn't speak our language which we had so eagerly developed and cultivated in Mexico. (Palacios, 2001, p. 55)

Es mi lengua
        Es mi lengua
y si tu no me entiendes
que te vaya bien, o que te vaya mal
        Es mi lengua
Conque ¿quieres que me conforme?
¿Por qué no te conformas tú?
        Es mi lengua
y si tu no me entiendes,
que te vaya bien o que te vaya mal
        Es mi lengua
¿Quién es quién? Tú me quieres decir...
más pronto salgo que entro
¿Por qué no me dejas vivir?
        Es mi lengua
Y si tu no me entiendes
que te vaya bien o que te vaya mal.
        Es mi lengua
(Poem translation)
It's my Language
It's my language, and if you don't understand me,
may it go well with you or may it go bad...
It's my language,
So you want me to conform?
Why don't you conform?
It's my language, and if you don't understand me,
may it go well with you or may it go bad...
It's my language.
Who's who? You want to tell me.
Yet no sooner I go out than come in
Why don't you let me live?
It's my language, and if you don't understand me,
may it go well with you or may it go bad...
It's my language.
Unpublished poem 1998, Ignacio Palacios

BORDER-ING

In the Brownsville, Texas, school what I remember most is my fifth grade teacher, Mr. White (pseudonyms used throughout), giving me a magazine to look at since I didn't know English.

"Raya tu nombre aquí," said my new Tex-Mex classmate.

"¿Qué?" Scratch your name here, I wondered . . . He was merely using his Spanglish to try to communicate to this newly arrived Mexican student, who had problems understanding his language. But as he communicated through gestures and words, and I finally understood, I did finally write my name on that sheet.

Mr. White didn't know what to do with me; though I had been literate in Spanish, could even recite poetry, now I was a dumb illiterate Mexican—excluded and silenced from this new "literacy club" (Smith, 1988). Though my Tex-Mex peers didn't make it any easier, by taunting me and making fun of me for not knowing their Tex-Mex, I stubbornly learned English by paying attention to oral language.

At recess, we would all go toward the school candy and snack store, a little wooden shed, for lack of vending machines. My parents had bought a candy bar for me which I really liked, but I couldn't pronounce its name in English: Zero. My classmates giggled at my feeble attempts, as I pronounced in Spanish, *cero*.

"Why don't you ask for me, since you know English already?"

"You need to learn English," they answered in their heavy Tex-Mex Spanish accent.

I was excluded from my classmates' world and from the teacher's world— my crime was not knowing their language!

Since I did know how to write Spanish already, I recall writing in *my own spelling* (as I perceived the words to be from my phonetic Spanish) formulaic phrases that I was beginning to recognize—*tenkyu (thank you), plis (please), yurlakam (you're welcome), uatsyurneim (what's your name?), jaolaryu (how old are you?)*, etc. I did eventually learn the proper spellings, however. I was being my own teacher, taking responsibility for my own learning, since my teacher neglected his duty! All he could do was give me a picture magazine to look at while the rest of the class had their lessons.

A sad occurrence in Brownsville, though, was that I was placed in kindergarten for summer school so I could learn to read and write, even though I was almost eleven! My parents, in their well-meaning but ignorant attempts at wanting me to get the "basics" of English, had requested I be placed in kindergarten for summer school. (I know my parents must have been going through their own culture shock and language learning experiences of their own. Maybe that is why they thought kindergarten would be a better place for me to begin!) In this kindergarten classroom I remember that since I was bigger than the rest of the children, the teachers also effectively ignored me in the classroom, saying they did not know what to do with me—they left me to merely look and listen. They must have hoped I would learn by osmosis (?).

I recall that on one occasion the other children were allowed to feel letters made of felt material pasted on construction paper, but I was not allowed to do so, because I was too old. I wondered what I was doing there, and I guess the teachers wondered the same thing. What was a fifth grader doing in kindergarten? Some literacy practices are quite exclusionary, instead of helping they may do more damage than good.

MORE REFLECTIONS ON CHANGE

The first thing evident is the cultural change my family and I had to undergo. In the middle of the twentieth century, America's *melting pot* concept was changed to the *salad bowl* idea, especially with the introduction of bilingual education in the U.S. in the late sixties and early seventies. Nonetheless, though this shift led to more inclusion and acceptance of minorities, many immigrants still faced social pressure to change language and culture. In my case, in the Southwest, there was pressure from the Tex-Mex culture for newly arrived Mexican immigrants to become Tex-Mex, and from the Anglo-American culture to become Anglicized. I believe the Southwest has the greatest Spanish language maintenance of any language/cultural group in the US. But, as I reflect on this, I am sad to say that in my early years I didn't want to be associated with the Tex-Mex culture — perhaps because I sensed the hostilities between the majority and the minority populations. According to Rosenbaum (1981), there is a historical legacy of hostility between the Tex-Mex and the Anglo cultures:

> The population of the United States includes a myriad of ethnic affiliations and cultural traditions. In general terms, however, all but three groups can be called voluntary citizens or residents. The three exceptions—Afro Americans, Native Americans, and Mexican Americans—are involuntary Americans because their inclusion in the country resulted from Anglo American aggression. (p. 5)

I didn't want to be seen as one belonging to the underclass, and in this respect I can identify with Richard Rodriguez (*Victim* , 1994) when he states he didn't want to associate with his Mexican culture. Rosenbaum (1981) says, "The separation of Tejas from Mexico. . . occurred in the context of extreme violence [in the early 1800s], and violence sanctioned by the Remember-the-Alamo myth characterized 'normal' interaction between Anglo and *mexicano* [sic] to a much greater extent than in either California or New Mexico" (p. 33) during the 19th century and early part of the 20th century. This legacy has left bitter feelings. Was I to become part of that legacy? I really didn't want to. Yet, what other options did I have? I had come as a child of immigrant parents; I was to become part of the Generation 1.5: not American by birth, but American by educational training.

IN-CORP-ORATION

The next school year, my family and I moved to Corpus Christi, Texas. We children were happier there, since it was a bigger city. My parents originally wanted the school officials in Corpus Christi, Texas, to place me in first grade, so that I could learn "inglés" better. Fortunately, because of my age, the school officials decided just to put me back only one grade. I was placed in fifth grade again, after having finished it in Brownsville, Texas. Whereas in Mexico I had been developing perfect literacy skills, in the U. S. I was always being told I couldn't be perfect enough for *Them.* I ponder now: was I a critical literate thinker like Baynham (1995) discusses? Was I beginning to question educational practices even in fifth grade? Baynham would say only critical literacies are best—those that question the established authority's literacy superimposed on the minority.

My parents were simply doing their best.

Again I rely on my dissertation to repeat ideas and words here that I deem appropriate to this autobiography:

> In Corpus Christi, I remember my parents began attending night English and citizenship classes. They too wanted the best that America had to offer. I recall their literacy/citizenship books. One particular story began thus: "My name is Jim Davis." It was about a white Anglo-Saxon American learning to be literate. My parents attended these evening classes after a long hard day at work. My father worked in a Texaco gas station pumping gas, while my mother worked in a bakery as the clerk selling Mexican bread. My parents wanted full participation/acceptance, so they thought about becoming American citizens. As I think about it now, I know they too had their own struggles with this new environment, and they wanted to fit in as well as they could. (Palacios, 2001, p. 56)

I remember helping my dad at the Texaco station some days, especially on my days off school. "One particular day" in 1969, "I crawled into the back seat of our old... station wagon - - exhausted after a long ten hour work-day! I know how father must have felt after working hard, then going to those evening classes and reading stories about a middle class American named Jim Davis. The elusive American Dream was appearing" (Palacios, 2001, p. 56) ... or was it vanishing?

THE IMPERFECT SEVEN AND LEARNING SPELLING

Here I can return to the imperfect seven story. It was in Corpus Christi, Texas, that my new fifth grade teacher was telling me that my letters and numbers were incorrectly written! I couldn't write the r as I had been taught ( ) because it would confuse people with an x, and I couldn't write the 7 crossed because it would confuse people with an F. Nothing made sense to me. I did wonder if people in the United States could be so dumb as to confuse a 7 with an f and an r with an x. How could that be? Anyway, I had to unlearn that literacy and numeracy practice I had been taught in Mexico, since supposedly people in the US would confuse such writing!

Not everything was negative, however. I recall that I began to associate spellings of words by sounding them out in Spanish. I learned to spell in English by sounding out all letters, since I was using my own Spanish phonetic system, and I amazed some of my friends! Here's how I was doing it. I would pronounce every English letter (as if written in Spanish) and memorize the word. For instance: C-O-M-P-L-I-A-N-C-E, I would pronounce sounding out all English letters as if it were a Spanish word: compliance (pronouncing the syllables *iance* as if all the letters had Spanish vowels, no silent *e*). I would then associate the word with its English pronunciation, and listened as the teacher dictated the spelling words. Since I already had memorized every letter, I would make hundreds on all my spelling tests. Moreover, it was the same fifth grade teacher, Mr. Rodriguez, the one correcting my sevens, who went to our house to sell us a *World Book Encyclopedia*, convincing my parents that it would help us learn English.

Unknowingly, though he was surely wanting to sell his merchandise, Mr. Rodriguez introduced me to a world of books, and I became an avid admirer of them through that encyclopedia and dictionary. The world of books opened up to me through the U. S. schools. I remember going to the school library and being amazed at all the books, and being able to check out books which I myself could choose! I was learning *inglés* and beginning to understand the magical code. I was becoming literate - - the secret was being unraveled for me! I recall my first book report in fifth grade in English. Mr. Rodriguez had suggested I check out a first grade book (I believe it was *Mary Had a Little Lamb*), and as I tried to read the pages and point to the pictures in front of the class, my peers giggled and snickered. At the time, I had begun to think it was because of my language inability in English; however, as I consider it in hindsight, I wonder whether it may have been both my language or lack of it, or whether it was my lack of socio-cultural knowledge of using appropriate age materials for fifth graders; I was using nursery rhymes, material intended for kindergarteners! Sociolinguistic and pragmatic knowledge was lacking.

Since I am the oldest child, my parents had always told me I was supposed to be a model, including in language use, to my siblings. Even my maternal grandfather, whom we grandchildren referred to as "Nano," had always encouraged us to learn English well because, as he said, "The bilingual person is worth two people." I remember I was supposed to help my brother and sister with their language problems, but actually we would all help each other. Also, my siblings and I were asked many times by my parents to translate documents and interpret for them into Spanish, so this language experience helped us to focus on learning the language well. We were made to become little adults representing our parents to the outside world. This scenario is played out many times in immigrant families. For instance, I remember one incident. We children were just learning some of the language, when we went to a Kentucky Fried Chicken restaurant. None of us children wanted to speak in public since we were very shy and afraid of making mistakes with our imperfect English. My father was adamant that I should make the order. Embarrassed, I said I couldn't, and became afraid of the consequences of my father's anger, punishment. My father (though never a violent man) got very mad and stomped out of the restaurant! We went to a drive in movie, but were left without our supper because of our lack of language skills; that—he said—was our punishment.

Chapter Six

Acculturation in America

DEVELOPING ENGLISH LITERACY

Our second year in the U. S., we moved to Chicago Heights, Illinois.

One day, Mrs. Perry, my sixth grade teacher at Garfield Elementary, wanted us to practice reading lines in a play. I was chosen to go forward and read some lines. I was extremely hesitant, knowing my English was still very poor. I mispronounced the word "school," pronouncing it as if it had Spanish vowels and saying instead something like the English word "skull." My classmates roared with laughter as I blushed. I didn't even know what I had done, for I didn't even know the word *skull*.

"Now, kids, you know Ignacio is just learning English. You need to remember that! Go on, Ignacio."

Embarrassed, I asked to be relieved of the responsibility.

However, during the next two years, I became very good in spelling and in language arts, even better than my English-speaking American peers, who seemed jealous of my achievements. I thought, at least if I learn this language and the language skills well, I can succeed in America. I didn't want to be labeled as a failure. I wanted to please my teachers, my reference group, since my peers were too unkind most of the time. I think teachers were some of my role models, and I wanted to join their club, especially since my peers left me out of theirs. In this respect, I resembled Richard Rodriguez when he uses the 'scholarship boy" metaphor—his quest of becoming like his authority figures, the teachers in his life (Rodriguez, 1982, p. 58).

REFLECTIONS ON CULTURAL CHANGE

Still, like many children of immigrants, I did go through cultural change from my native culture to the host culture. It was especially when we moved to Chicago Heights, Illinois, that I began to feel that I was becoming "American." In fact, in sixth grade, when we were discussing the Civil War, I sensed that it was better to be from the North, the winning side, so I too made fun of the "southerners" and their speech patterns, laughing along with my classmates at the "funny" southern accents (whereas I had been the object of ridicule before, now I was joining in the ridicule).

I remember in seventh grade my cultural ambivalence, not wanting my mother to send corn taco tortillas with *carne asada* (charbroiled strips of meat—which I loved) for lunch since I had to bite at it kind of awkwardly, and I was embarrassed for my peers to see I didn't have something like their white bread with cold meat sandwiches. It got to the point I asked Mother not to send me any more lunches, and I started just buying ice cream sandwiches for lunch, since I really didn't care to buy the foul smelling meatloaf in the cafeteria!

My parents, however, didn't assimilate as easily; they had not continued with their English classes since we had moved to Chicago Heights. Perhaps they had left their ambitions of becoming American citizens behind. Though we children were being assimilated through school, my parents were not.

I HAVE A NIGHTMARE!

In 1970, we were shown a documentary in one of my seventh grade classes. A black man kept repeating a phrase: "I have a dream!" Students were getting stirred in our seventh grade. I was unaware of any political news, but could sense black students wanted to rise up and protest, for some unknown reason to me.

"You can't come in here," several black students stood in front of the school door and denied any entrance to any non-black student. I tried another door, but some other groups of students were standing in front of each door to Washington Junior High and obstructing entrance to the building. I wondered, "Why did that Black man have a dream? Was it to keep us non-Blacks from participating in education? Some school officials finally got word of the protest and obstruction and dispersed the students. Martin Luther King's dream appeared like a nightmare to me that day, as I fearfully attended classes that day, where all of God's children couldn't walk hand in hand, no matter their color.

I BE, YOU BE, HE BE — A LESSON IN EBONICS?

The next year in eighth grade, on one occasion I stood outside the school building door, waiting for the bell to ring, so I could enter the building after lunch and return to classes.

"Why you be here?" A Black student asked me, as I looked at him perplexed and afraid, remembering what had happened the year before.

"I'm sorry, I don't understand," I answered as I moved a little further away from the door.

"Why you be here?" He was adamant.

"I'm waiting for the bell to ring so I can go into the building and go to my class."

"No, I mean, why you be here. Every day, you be here. Why you not move to another place?"

"Uh?" I couldn't understand his dialect, having recently learned standard English.

"All the time you be here," he answered.

"Oh, this is usually where I stand before the bell rings." My first encounter of the durative "be" verb, in Afro-English was a rather humorous encounter. Boy, did I have many more dialects to decipher in English!

REACHING FOR THE HEIGHTS

Since my teenage years I have been very much interested in languages and linguistics. As a teenager, I learned to read articles in the World Book Encyclopedia and once I tried unsuccessfully to read through the dictionary. I was a lover of words, a teenage philologist, if you will, which was rather odd for a teenager, but I dreamed about being a language and linguistics teacher! I thought about just dropping out of school and becoming self-educated by reading through the entire encyclopedia (I had read an article about how a person could become self-taught, just by reading the right books). One time I encountered an article about linguistics in the encyclopedia and thought it would be fascinating to know the phonetic alphabet. I remember inventing my own alphabet, a secret code language that I taught my brother and sister, and we would communicate in writing in this secret language! I started by doubling up printed letters in one way or another, creating my own code. DOLEALA, I called it—double letter alphabet language. Then I came up with another language, INDOLEALA, inverted double letter alphabet language. And since we all knew Spanish, we could do this in English or Spanish, which became even more of a cryptic language. I could do something others couldn't! I had secret power—my own literacy skills! The word was giving me power. I secretly cherished the dream that I would someday become a linguist! Then I wondered what it would be like to know many languages...

I recall that in sixth grade in 1969, my friend Ivano, a recent Italian immigrant, was also struggling with learning English, so we could identify with each other, and his mother and mine worked in the same frozen-pizza factory in Chicago Heights. Once in a while, Josephina would fix lasagna and bring some to our home. The smell of freshly baked lasagna filled our upstairs garage apartment. As she often would, Josephina would rattle off something in Italian trying to make herself understood, and amazingly mother and she could communicate, part in Spanish, part in Italian, and the other part in broken English! *Mama mia in la cocina*! I thought I wanted to learn Italian, too! (Years later in college, I did take Spanish for native speakers and French as a foreign language. When I left college for a couple of years, I studied Italian on my own, using a Berlitz book.)

In sixth grade I had done a report on Czechoslovakia and the 1968 communist takeover, and to my amazement, I happened to have a Czechoslovakian teacher in seventh grade! She greatly encouraged me in my language and writing experience. For one assignment we were supposed to write our autobiographies, and I told her that I didn't want to write about myself because it was too embarrassing to write about oneself. I didn't want to tell about my relatives in Mexico or my beautiful Monterrey with its Cerro de la Silla (Saddle Hill). But my teacher encouraged me to do it, so I wrote of how I missed living in my "Little Chicago," as Monterrey was known.

The second semester, as part of language arts class, we were all supposed to try to write plays, so (based on characters I had gleaned from a Scholastic book about ghosts) I wrote a skit entitled, DR. FREAKY, WHO IS REALLY FREAKY!—a comedy skit about a modern psychotherapist (Dr. Freaky) whose patients are all monsters—a vampire, a werewolf, a mummy, a witch. The plot of the story was that Dr. Freaky wanted to hurry up and finish his day at the office seeing patients, so he could get back to work on his secret monster making project (Frank and Stein). With my teacher's consent, I included scattered through the skit some of the Scholastic book poems about monsters.

To my surprise, the teacher chose my skit, along with several other skits, to type up and distribute it to the class. I was thrilled to see my story in print! Then the class voted to perform my skit for another class. I was elated! I thought, "I guess I can really write!" She encouraged me to write, saying maybe I could be a writer some day! On the day the skit was supposed to be performed for another class, one of the main characters decided he'd play hooky and goofed off in the hall. Meanwhile, as I watched the play being performed and my classmate did not return, when I knew it was his turn to come in, I stood up and bravely and unexpectedly walked in front of the class and started playing his part. My other classmates in the play figured out that I was improvising, taking over the absent classmate's part, and we wonderfully played along until the play was finished! They later congratulated me not only for writing the skit, but also saving the day, playing one of the parts on the spot! I remembered my part in the stage play in Monterrey, Mexico, *Disonancias*, in which I played the role of a small page. Language and drama were coming back to envelope me!

Encouragement from teacher and classmates affected me positively. From that time on I thought I would try to write stories or plays, remembering my days in Mexico and my father's work in theater, and my grandmother's stories about monsters and ghouls. My seventh grade Czechoslovakian teacher had the greatest influence in my learning to love reading and writing, both in school and for pleasure.

Would-Be Writer

As a teenager, I spent many hours typing stories in English—not only for school assignments, but for pleasure. Yet none of my teachers knew I was writing for myself, just for pleasure. Though I didn't know how to type, I told my Dad I wanted to be a writer.

"Quiero ser escritor, Papi."

"Tienes que estudiar mucho y leer mucho para ser escritor, sabes."

Yes I knew I had to read and study a lot to become a writer. Still, father bought me a manual portable typewriter. Perhaps the fact that words are printed on a page left an indelible impression on my mind that words were important if they were written down in type. I guess I pictured a writer as someone hunched over a typewriter, typing away. I had seen in a *Twilight Zone* episode a show about a writer whose characters live their own lives in their stories while the writer types away at a typewriter. I, too, pictured my characters having their own lives, living apart from my own stories—living characters! (I still have some of those stories I wrote.) Once, I used the glossary from my eighth grade literature book to try to use as many words from the glossary as I could in my story! I wanted to choose the words that had to do with horror—I wrote a "horror" story about someone being scared at night and "bashing" a creature's head in as the creature tried to attack him. The creature was merely a mosquito! I recall taking my stories to school to share with my teen-age classmates so they could read them, and they thought the stories were creative, though zany. And of course they would often point out my incorrect usage of words, such as "bashing" or "janitor" instead of groundskeeper. My eighth grade language arts teacher never knew about my writing outside of class at all! I recollect her commenting on an in class assignment (how to do something) that I was clever, since I had written about how to get rid of a vampire! But my in class writing was nothing compared to what I was attempting to do as I typed with two fingers in the evenings at home.

Another creative story I remember writing was about a boy stealing something out of his brother's chest of drawers during the early morning hours as they got ready for school. It was a suspense until the end—the stolen thing was a clean pair of socks!

For a class assignment in ninth grade, I wrote a myth, "Pylous of Mega," about a demigod hero who would fight off giant bats and rescue his maiden from some enchanted place and both would return to his homeland to be king of Mega. Though I made an A, my high school teacher wrote a comment about it being too long!

That was the end of my attempts at writing much of anything.

I felt that my days as a writer were ended because my private pleasurable experience in writing and my public academic school writing experience conflicted! In my out of school writing I could write whatever I wanted; while in public school, I had to merely follow the teacher's assignments. I wonder why educators don't just tap into students' own interests and use them as natural resources for reading and writing? I did love to learn and wanted very much to go to college, but certain personal turmoil during my teenage years (which I discuss later) led me to drop out of high school, though I deeply regretted it at the time.

WHAT AMERICA MEANT TO ME IN 1972

In 1972, while a freshman at Bloom Township High in Chicago Heights, I wrote the following essay for a school assignment. It illustrates my ambivalence in becoming bicultural then. That is why I have chosen to include it as a handwritten manuscript — showing my actual voice in ninth grade, around fourteen years old. This essay is written in English, four years after our immigration to the United States. It does show command of English language, though some ambivalence of cultural ties and identity.

REFLECTIONS ON CULTURAL CHANGE

When my family decided to move from Chicago Heights back to the Texas Rio Grande Valley, I certainly did not want to go back to Texas. I resented

What America Means to Me

I am not an American. I was born and brought up the first years of my life in Mexico. That is why it might be hard for me to really be honest in what I say. I choose this topic to write on because I can write the good and bad sides of it. If I had chosen one of the other two, it might really have been hard for me to be honest on what I would have said.

Now – to start. There are many good things in America which are good for the whole world. For example: Americans were first to walk on the moon; Americans have a system of social security and public welfare; almost everything in the United States is modern and almost futuristic.

But, not everything is cotton and daisies. Like many countries it too had many presidents assassinated. It has been in and out of wars. And not all people live happy there.

Also there is quite a bit of discrimination. There is discrimination towards chicanos, blacks, and American Indians. The WASP's think they're the greatest. Maybe they've been complemented too much. That's why I don't like to speak too highly about Americans, they might get too pampered.

I know this paper will not win any prize, it will not even get nominated. But at least I know that what I have written is truly honest and is the best I can say. No more I will say.

Figure 6.1. What America Meant to Me in 1972

having to be associated with Tex-Mex. I was becoming bicultural, but not necessarily Tex-Mex. I know when I was younger I wanted to be associated with Mexican immigrants more than with people born in the Tex-Mex culture. Yet I definitely cannot say with Rodriguez, "I'm not Mexican-American. I don't know what that means" (*Victim*, 1994). I *do* know. I view myself as having become and becoming Mexican-American. I am a Mexican immigrant becoming American. Today I have learned to accept stereotypes that are put on a minority person by the majority class. I am at ease with certain cultural tensions I felt I suffered as a young teen-ager, as my manuscript above illustrates.

TODOS ANDÁBAMOS CORTANDO RÁBANOS, (WE ALL WENT ABOUT PICKING RADISHES) TITLE OF A POPULAR MEXICAN FIELD LABORER SONG

One of the cultural drawbacks in returning to the Rio Grande Valley was the fact that we went from a suburban town near Chicago, Illinois, to the backwoods of southwest Texas, a tiny town known as Roma, Texas. While we lived there it seemed to my brothers and sister and me that we had gone back in time. There were dusty dirt roads, and a tiny three room apartment for the six of us (my baby brother had been born in Chicago).

For a short while I had to go to high school in a very small school and in the summers had to work in the fields, picking produce, melons, tomatoes, bell peppers, etc. This was work we were totally un-accustomed to, backbreaking work, for the migrants, which we thought was for the lowest of the poor! That's what we had become…

I remember the first time I had to carry on my back a sack of cantaloupes, while I bent down picking the fruit, and tossing it into the back sack. The heavy burden only got heavier as the sun rose and got hotter during the summer day. We worked in the fields only a few weeks, but we were finally fulfilling the minority migrant stereotype of the Mexican Americans working in the fields in Texas.

For a short while, we moved to Houston, Texas. We were all happier since it was a bigger city, not a rural area, yet my parents suffered for lack of steady work.

SAVING SOULS

Now, unlike Richard Rodriguez who claims he "lost [his] soul in America" because "ethnicity is related to the soul" (*Victim*, 1994), I don't believe I have lost my soul or sense of identity. Nonetheless, when I was about fifteen years old, I was going through an adolescent crisis that caused me to drop out of school.

Fatso! That's what I had been called since a child—genetically predisposed to being overweight. But it was too humiliating and embarrassing when in tenth grade I discovered I had to be in swimming in gym class. I had to endure enough taunts from my peers in the shower room and in the other gym classes, but having to get into swimming trunks, exposing my fat belly, would have been too humiliating, I thought. It bothered me so much that I detested going to school and tried to avoid going to gym class.

In the early 1990s as I resided in Florida, I read an article in the Palm Beach Post about a twelve year old young boy who actually committed suicide in the summer rather than face junior high class mates the next school year; he left a note saying he didn't want to go to school, since he knew he was going to be made fun of, especially in gym class because of his weight! It reminded me of my own emotional turmoil in high school.

"You have to take this class in order to graduate," were the counselor's words as I sat in his office.

"I really wanted to take typing instead," I pleaded.

"You'll have to drop some other class, but you have to take gym class!" That was the torturous world I had to endure—or so I thought.

Emotional turmoil engulfed me—this is a chapter of my life I have never disclosed to anyone, but now feel I must share it in order to help others see the emotional torture that peer pressure does produce. I loved school and wanted to go on to college some day, and even become a linguistics scholar, but here was a terrible emotional burden I could not handle, and I could not let anyone know my inner and spiritual battles. How could I undress and wear swimming trunks as the coach had demanded?

One morning on my way to school, in emotional distress, crying every step of the way, I decided I could not take it any more. I went by the American Catholic church (which we did not attend), to where I assumed was the priest's parsonage. I was in tears and wanting to explain the situation to the priest whom I thought would help me.

The door opened. A nun was shocked to see me in tears right in her front door. I don't know what she thought when I sobbed, " I don't want to go to school. I want to talk to the priest."

Extremely frightened at seeing me crying right in her front door, she told me to go on to the next house, which was the priest's. Startled that this was not the priest, and upset as I was, I wondered whether she was so scared she would call the police on me or something, so I just walked on out of her sight, severely depressed and disappointed, and headed back to the street, instead of walking to where she had directed me. I headed over to the house where we were living with some friends. In our friends' house in Houston, we had made a bedroom out of an old back porch.

"Why didn't you go to school today?" My father demanded to know when he came back from work. I didn't have a real answer, so I said I was not feeling well.

"I need a note today from you saying I was sick yesterday, Papá."

"Yo no te la voy a dar." He didn't believe I was sick, so he was not going to give me the note.

Mother had pity on me and wrote the lie on the note, just so I could go to school that day. It was not a day for gym class, so I could endure, but didn't know how much longer.

At that time, my family and I had been living in our family friends' back porch which had been converted into a back bedroom—all six of us! But around that crisis time, we had just moved into our own house, a few blocks away, an empty house, bare of any furniture, where we slept on mattresses on the floor.

My spiritual and emotional trauma was unbearable. One evening, I wrote a note to my parents, saying I couldn't take it any more, but I did not want to go to school to be made fun of. Crying, I handed the note to mother and locked myself in the bathroom. Though Mother tried to get me to come on out, I had found Papa's pain pills in the bathroom and had decided to end my life, so fearfully I took some pain pills — fortunately not enough to kill me, just to numb me, and calm my sobbing.

I was still locked in the bathroom when Papá came home and begged me to get out of the bathroom. All of us were emotionally distraught. In tears Papá hugged me, realizing what I had tried to do, and assured me I wouldn't have to go to school any more.

I loved school.

We moved away from the neighborhood, and I had told the school officials we were moving, so I needed transfer papers. I never went back to any school in the new neighborhood, or any other neighborhood. Though I longed to learn and become a teacher, I had locked myself out of the educational process because of my distress over my weight. And I couldn't tell anyone in authority in the school system. I attempted taking some correspondence courses to get my GED, but that also came to naught because of lack of finances.

Yet redemption came my way. I had a spiritual conversion in Houston, Texas, and became part of an American Christian church that my family and I were attending. In the community of church people, we met the first group of American Anglos that accepted us just for who we were. Rodriguez, though outspokenly rejecting his ethnic background, still does say "You can be born again in America," referring mainly to a redeeming cultural change (Victim, 1994). But in America, in the English church community of people, I experienced a spiritual re-birth. Also, I felt acceptance and appreciation—a validation of who I was, just as I was.

> Just as I am,
> tho' tossed about
> With many a conflict,
> many a doubt,
> Fightings and fears
> within, without,
> O Lamb of God,
> I come! I come!
> (Third Stanza of Popular Gospel Song written by Charlotte Elliott, 1789-1871)

MY DREAM—TO TEACH

"Would anyone be interested in helping us teach Vacation Bible School (VBS)?" asked Sister Donna, the pastor's wife.

"Could I help?" I was only sixteen, and recently converted.

"Yes, you can teach a class if you want to." She was trying to encourage me. I felt thrilled to have been given such a responsibility and trust.

I taught the eight to ten year olds, what would have been Sister Donna's own class! The Pastors were showing love and concern for this Mexican immigrant, trusting that such an inexperienced fellow could lead twenty little ones through a week of VBS! To my surprise our class won the award for the highest attendance! That experience gave me confidence and satisfaction and an inner belief that maybe I could be a teacher someday. My dream was reborn.

I feel my church experience is an overall asset to my cultural learning experience because through my participation in church settings I have learned much about American culture and society. Our frequent invitations to the parsonage provided me one view into American culture: social life, food, games, humor. I remember at first the strangeness being in a white Anglo-American's home for the first time. We ate cookies, played table games, and enjoyed laughter and fun. I thought it was very nice of them to invite us, and we wanted to stay for the rest of the evening

"You're welcome to sleep here, but we don't have room for everybody!" Pastor Robert joked. Thus, the differences in cultures were apparent between our family and theirs, one following Mexican time, the other American. But it was a genuinely positive experience. I loved the pastor and wanted to become like him someday!

Therefore, the church community of people since then has been one of my primary acculturation places in the U. S. In the church community I have found "a club" that accepts me, just as I am. Redemption came my way — a new life, a new opportunity!

> Nazco
> Nazco   I am born.
> The recesses of my mind reach
> for memories repressed
> Not allowed to be born.
> Regular memories never remembered.
> Nazco   I am born.
> Once there, in another place, in another time.
> Then here, in this place, at this time.
> Rocking my memory back and forth until I'm born. . .
> Nazco.   The fury of being born.
> The recollections never told. I am born.
> Nazco   Am I born?
> He came and delivered me not then
> but again;
>   now born I am
> The recesses of my mind reach
> for memories repressed
> Now allowed. . .   now born.
> Nazco,   born, again.   Unpublished Poem 1998 Ignacio Palacios

INTERLUDE — BACK IN MEXICO

My parents, however, were not happy with my conversion, so they sent me back to live with my grandmother and study in Mexico for a school year, 1974-1975. My parents moved to Brownsville, Texas, while I lived with my relatives for that year.

As I was attending the training school for teachers, I remember one instance when one teacher asked me where I was from, and I answered "Brownsville," pronouncing the word in English, and the teacher mocked me repeating the English pronunciation in an exaggerated fashion, making fun of me. I was saying it correctly, but my teacher wanted me to pronounce it in the Spanish pronunciation "Bronsbil," instead of Brownsville. Now, where was I to fit in? I recalled in Chicago being made fun of my English mispronunciation of "school," and now I was a foreigner in my own country of Mexico!

Though I was still a Mexican citizen, the Mexicans now saw me as the *Tejano, del otro lado*.

One good happening while I studied in the Normal, was that the English teacher exempted me from taking tests, once she found out I was perfectly fluent in English.

"Do you speak English, Ignacio? "

"Yes, I do. I have lived in Chicago and in Texas. I have gone to school in the United States."

One time she was teaching the word "finger," and told the class that the fingers were also those on the feet! I corrected her and told her that on our feet we have toes, but fingers on our hands only. She consulted with another teacher and decided I was right!

She was impressed. She asked me to help her teach the English class some times, even to help my classmates with their project of writing skits in English. I was involved helping all the small groups writing their skits in English. My world of writing and drama had come to me again!

BACK TO TEXAS

For various reasons my parents brought me back to live with them again, this time, back to Roma, Texas, where I worked picking produce once more during the fall and winter of 1975. I still recall the backbreaking work picking tomatoes on cold December mornings.

We left the house at five-thirty or six each morning, since we had to catch a ride in the back of a pick-up truck and be in the fields by six-thirty. Sometimes, though we were required to be on hand by six-thirty am, we wouldn't be put to work until around 9:30 or 10:00am, for the field bosses said the tomatoes were still too frozen to pick, so they made us wait, without pay. Other times, we would work for a couple of hours only, then we were sent back home—about $1.85 per hour, for only two hours of work—the injustice was evident, especially since the minimum wage was $2.10 per hour. Oh, but field laborers were seen as only scum, so easily dispensed with if they got tired of the meager and unjust working conditions.

    Piscando Tomates

Viento helado,
Diciembre frío.
Espalda encorvada,
Manoseando tomates.
Piscaba uno,
Verde durito,

Fresco, lisito.
Ramas espinozas,
Verdes del tomate,
Picando las manos.
El pie pisando,
Uno rojo podrido.
Chillaba lágrimas,
Rojas, negras.
Adolorido, muriendo.
Callado y silencioso
Eco angustioso.
Mugrosa cara,
Polvo en las narices.
Espalda adolorida,
Piscando tomates.
Diciembre frío.
Viento helado.

Picking Tomatoes

Frozen wind,
Cold December.
Bent back,
Handling tomatoes.
Picking one,
Green firm.
Fresh, smooth.
Thorny branches.
Green, of the tomato,
Stinging the hands.
The foot stepping on
A red rotten one.
Crying tears.
Red, black.
Aching, dying.
Not speaking and silent.
Anguished echo.
Dirty face.
Dust in the nose.
Aching back.
Picking tomatoes.
Cold December.
Frozen wind.   Unpublished poem 2006, Ignacio Palacios

HISTORIA DE AMOR: LOVE STORY

During the fall of 1975, I underwent another turmoil emotionally. When I had gotten converted in Houston, I had had a crush on a young lady, older than I was, with whom I had been corresponding for a year or so during my stay in Monterrey and now in Texas. Probably because she was older than I was, and probably because she was Anglo-Saxon Protestant, my parents vehemently objected to our relationship, at that time.

"Ya no queremos que le escribas a Cynthia, y no queremos que leas esas revistas de la iglesia!" I was shocked—I was not to write to her anymore, nor even read my church periodical?

I had a big argument with my parents that night. I walked out of the three room apartment with a pile of Cynthia's letters and my church periodicals, going toward the back yard where the trash cans were. I dumped them all, heart-broken. But instead of walking back into the apartment, I kept walking out to the dusty road. Sobbing and devastated, I walked on and on. My sister Gracie drove up to meet me some blocks away from the house.

"Get in the car, Nacho."

"No, I'm not going back home."

"Where are you going?"

"I don't know, but I'm leaving."

"Nacho, don't do that. Come back home."

" Gracie, let me go. I'm going around the town."

She let me go on walking. I literally went around to the north side, then to the west side of that little town. I went south, then back east. I walked around the entire perimeter. I had left in the afternoon; now it was getting dark. I guess I'll walk on to Rio Grande City, I was thinking. Around eight or nine that evening, my sister drove up again as I was heading east.

"Where are you going, Nacho?"

"I don't know. Rio Grande, I guess." I was more calmed down.

My sister convinced me to come on back to the apartment. I really had no where else to go, and no money to go anywhere anyway. So, I did go back home with her.

No one in the family said much as I got myself ready for bed, with pain in my heart.

It was about that time that my parents encouraged me to go to college. I guess they were trying to get me distracted from Cynthia and from my church association. Since I had already dropped out of high school, and had not finished my training in Mexico, I obtained my GED and enrolled at the local Pan American University (now University of Texas-Pan American) for the spring of 1976. Going to college was a process that changed the course of my destiny. Instead of picking tomatoes for the rest of my life, I was picking courses to take at the local university.

During college I resumed my correspondence with Cynthia (who years later was to become my wife), and I continued to receive the church periodicals.

Cynthia had decided she was going to become a missionary in Mexico. I had wondered why she was doing that... why not get married and have a family . . . instead of her insane idea of adopting a child as a single woman!

"I'm coming to study Spanish in the Rio Grande Valley," she wrote to me.

I was thrilled! But now she was to become a missionary, while I had barely started with my first year of college. A complex set of problems started to develop. How could our relationship ever work? She was to be a missionary in Mexico—I, a college student in Texas. Were we to continue corresponding? She came for a semester in 1976, because she wanted to be close to me. I loved that, but I could not relate to her very well, the missionary, older than I was, with a clear sense of purpose and direction, whereas I didn't even know yet what I was going to major in.

Her heart sank because I didn't say I loved her. She literally became physically sick because of the turmoil, being around me, and neither of us being able to express our love. She went back up north to be treated for illness. I was confused.

"Why don't you ask her to be your girlfriend?" I had asked my roommate. "No, she's too pure. Why don't you ask her?" He knew I liked her.

One day, as I was walking home from the university, I saw a red car parked in front of our apartment. I ran to see Cynthia. I was elated! My roommate noticed my eagerness and knew I was in love. Why didn't I know it? He laughed as I went to greet Cynthia. She was happy to see me also, but just wanted to ask if she could drop off some of her belongings and leave them in our apartment while she went to Mexico to be a missionary. My heart sank! She is leaving after all. Could we continue this relationship? I decided we could only be friends... she wasn't very happy. She went to become a missionary. We corresponded off and on for a few months, but finally I gave up. This isn't going to work, I thought, so I stopped writing to her.

Around that time, my Uncle Chuy in Monterrey died, which was an emotional time for all. When he died and we were in Monterrey, my mother asked me to write to Cynthia and inform her that Uncle Chuy had died. I wrote to Cynthia as my own mother had requested, a request I never thought would be made. Cynthia came to Monterrey from San Fernando, Tamaulipas, to sympathize with the bereaved, but it was a refreshingly new getting re-acquainted time.

After my Uncle's death and funeral, my parents decided to move to California, to go picking in the fields and work in the produce processing plants. I left college and joined them. My sister Gracie became ill with cancer, then leukemia. She died there. But the California experience for one year is a totally different story, so I will save it for another time.

Only one conversation with my mother's young cousin who was my own age stands out related to my love story.

"Do you have a girlfriend?" asked Joe, my second cousin.

"No." I replied.

"Why not?"

"I just write to a missionary friend in Mexico sometimes."

The question, "Why not?" really made me ponder, indeed, why couldn't I ask Cynthia to be my girlfriend? I wrote to her concerning the idea, but at that time Cynthia had decided she had to write me off her life, as she endeavored to be a missionary in Mexico, and because I was far away in California. Our lives would take some twists and turns, but suffice it to say, after my sister died, and we went to bury her in Monterrey, Cynthia also came, and it was a time for more serious considerations about our growing friendship. Eventually, I transferred my college credits to a Bible college in Kansas City, and I finally did marry this Anglo-American woman. Thus, I became integrated into American life even more intimately.

Chapter Seven

Metamorphosis

THE CULTURAL, LINGUISTIC, AND IDENTITY METAMORPHOSIS

For this section, again I rely on my own dissertation to repeat ideas and words here which I deem appropriate for my autobiography (indented paragraphs since I quote at length):

> Ulla Connor (1999) in her description of how she learned academic discourses and became a writer in English as her second language, mentions her transformation, which I call metamorphosis, into an American citizen. When it comes to psycho-social identity and cultural change, I also experienced the ambivalence and anomie of identity crisis and metamorphosis. Connor, describing her experiences in writing during a sabbatical in Finland (which she subtitles "End of Journey"), says she realized then that she really wasn't Finnish in her approach at writing or viewing and reporting knowledge. She realized this when her suggestions about rewriting were ignored by her Finnish colleagues. "I guess I was completely Americanized because no major changes based on my suggestions were included in the final version of the Finnish booklet. In addition, the Finns perceived my oral presentation as well as my writing skills as quite typically those of a United States speaker . . . This experience and many others in Finland during my sabbatical last year encouraged me to apply for U. S. citizenship" (p. 35-36). Ulla Connor has undergone this metamorphosis, as I have.
>
> I remember how awkward I felt one time when I lived in Mexico as a married adult (1983-1985), a foreign missionary in my native country of Mexico. I had gone to a government office to make arrangements to have taxes waived for street paving on a church property, since by Mexican law all church buildings belonged to the government, and as a consequence are technically exempt from

taxes on public works. Anyway, my gestalt moment occurred when the woman who was interviewing me asked, "Where are you from?"

I answered, "I'm from Monterrey."

She asked, "Are you American?"

"No, I'm Mexican, why?"

"You sound like a foreigner. Have you spent a lot of time with Americans?"

"Yes."

"Maybe that's why you don't sound Mexican!"

When I returned to the U. S. after my missionary service, I went on to get my MA in ESL and became a teacher of English in the U. S. (Palacios, 2001, p. 57)

A complete re-birth had occurred! Again, I quote my own dissertation for the following:

> The story of my acquisition of academic discourse has been occurring since my days in college. Growing up in the United States, most of my educational experiences had already prepared me for the academic expectations in college. Of course, I remember the composition course, the rhetoric course, the literature courses, etc., in my undergraduate work. I had been invited to join the Honors Classes. I had been enthralled by the world literature class learning about the major works—*The Odyssey, The Iliad, The Inferno*, etc. I had read about *The Will of Zeus* and *The Mask of Jove*. I learned about Western Civilization, the Reformation, etc. Throughout college, I had been in the process of becoming an American already without realizing it. (Palacios, 2001, p. 58)

Then again, my college and graduate studies also were "teaching me academic discourse. I was doing well, even in writing papers and taking exams" (Palacios, 2001, p. 58). I was even hired as a TA to teach English at Pan American University. Here's an occurrence from my dissertation, which I repeat:

> One day, as I taught my English Composition class, one of my Mexican-American instructors with whom I was taking a sociology class in American Minorities saw me teaching.
>
> "I saw you teaching English as I walked down the hall the other day."
>
> "Yes, I teach English."
>
> "I can't believe that a Mexican citizen is teaching English in an American university!" He said publicly in our sociology class. This episode and other events like it made me realize I was more American now than Mexican. It was through these experiences in my adult life that I decided to apply for American citizenship. (Palacios, 2001, p. 58)

I was now a Mexican immigrant re-born as an American citizen —two languages and two cultures intermingled. This process has been re-occurring

Figure 7.1. Mexican flag

many times to other migrants since the time the Aztecs left Aztlan (the US Southwest) in search for a home place (Tenochtitaln, Mexico). Following my generational ascent, now I was back in Aztlan, the American Southwest.

Anzaldúa (1987) says that "the struggle of identities continues, the struggle of borders is our reality still. One day the inner struggle will cease and true integration take place" (p. 85). I don't know about Anzaldúa's integration, but I believe I have found integration for my own self. The following poem illustrates the metaphor of my own life.

El Águila y La Serpiente
El águila y la serpiente
sobre un nopal se treparon
"¡Este nopal yo lo quiero!"
dijo el águila a la serpiente
"Como mío vine a enroscarme
aunque antes no lo fue
del indígena ya era antes que yo viniera"

Figure 7.2. US flag

"¡Pues para mí, yo lo quiero!"
Se pusieron a luchar
El águila vino del norte
Y del sur la serpiente...
Herida mortal le dio
el águila a la serpiente
Mientras ésta la mató
cuando la vívora le entró al vientre.
Ahora el águila herida
renueva toda su fuerza
pues dentro d'ella lleva
la estampa de la serpiente
Y aunque a Tenochtitlan se comió
la serpiente y el águila la mató,
muy dentro de su vientre
el águila lleva ahora
la estampa de la serpiente
América se llama el águila,
Aztlan, la serpiente.

Figure 7.3. Eagle and Serpent

The Eagle and the Serpent
The eagle and the serpent
climbed up atop the cactus
"This cactus I want!"
said the eagle to the serpent
"As if it were mine I came to entwine myself in it,
though it wasn't mine to begin with,
it belonged to the Indian before I arrived."
"Well, I want it for me!"
And they began to wrestle
The eagle came from the North,
And from the South, the serpent. . .
A mortal wound the eagle gave unto the serpent
While the former killed it, the serpent entered into its belly.
Now the wounded eagle
recovers all its strength
for inside it has
the seal of the serpent
And though the serpent ate Tenochtitlan
And the eagle killed it,
deep inside its belly
the eagle now has
the seal of the serpent
America is the eagle,
Aztlan the serpent

Unpublished poem, 1998, Ignacio Palacios

I read Gloria Anzaldúa's (1987)) autobiography *Borderlands: La Frontera* in 2006 and discovered that like other Mexican authors, she also discusses the eagle and the serpent, a typical symbol of Mexico. She says the following about the bilingual bicultural experience of the Mexican-American:

> We distinguish between mexicanos del otro lado and mexicanos de este lado. Deep in our hearts we believe that being Mexican has nothing to do with which country one lives in. Being Mexican is a state of soul — not one of mind, not one of citizenship. Neither eagle nor serpent, but both. And like the ocean, neither animal respects borders. (p. 84)

I, however, need to append that though the eagle and the serpent is my own metaphor for my bilingual bicultural experience, I am now a new creation — a bridge between two languages and cultures. The bilingual bicultural person can reach out and extend both arms to both languages and cultures, and thus become a bridge for cultural and linguistic understanding.

Chapter Eight

Current Literacies

MY CURRENT LITERACY

For this section, I am again repeating ideas and words I have in my dissertation. "We all carry around many literacies, some blurring into one another. Though people's lives are filled with lived experiences in many unacknowledged literacies," my many literacies in English and Spanish, including in Christianity and the Bible, "could be mostly ignored in academic contexts" (Palacios, 2001, p. 60). Today, however, as an adult in the church work I do, I find myself speaking and writing in Spanish—sermon outlines, sermons, Bible studies, letters, church manuals, etc. (My Spanish biblical literacy I had to learn on my own when I was a missionary in Mexico, which is another story in itself!). As a teacher, I write in English—proposals, committee minutes, memos, brochures, tests, and my lecture notes (both on transparency outlines, powerpoint presentations, and on paper). "At times I even try to write a poem or two when I feel inspired, especially after taking the class Teaching Writing in which we as teachers of writing were encouraged to write along with our students" (Palacios, 2001, p. 60).

Though I have been an adjunct professor of English and Spanish in public colleges and universities off and on, I have taught both internationals and American students in a small Christian college most of my professional life since 1989. I teach ESL, composition, TESOL Methods, Grammar for TESOL, TESOL theory, Descriptive Linguistics, and Spanish for Non-native speakers. In the Spanish Bible Institute in which I have been involved from time to time, I am called upon occasionally to teach basic writing courses in Spanish, public speaking in Spanish, etc. Additionally, I have taught adult Sunday school classes in Spanish at my local church. In all these contexts, I want students to appreciate the opportunity they have in literacy. I know that literacy is more than just reading/writing; it involves critical thinking skills. Yet, in the midst of helping them achieve critical literacies and academic literacies, whether they be in English as a second or first language, or in Spanish as a second or first language, or in biblical literacy, I endeavor to show care and concern for my students for who they are. I know I'm not perfect, and I have made many blunders in my teaching, but I try not to shatter my students' faith, just because I'm teaching critical literacies or academic literacies. On the contrary, I want to help them come up to the level *they* desire in academics. I do not want to deride my ESL students when they write drafts or do prewriting in Chinese or Japanese; I do not want them to feel that their language is not good, or that their sevens are imperfect, or their beliefs are imperfect. I only want to help them see that English, especially writing, can be an asset for them, not a burden. The same is true of my teaching of Spanish.

I have had many experiences in the Christian college and in my Sunday School class which have given me opportunity to help my students learn different literacies, especially in background knowledge and cross-cultural differences. I will share some examples which illustrate the language and culture connection in L2 and C2 (language two and culture two) acquisition.

A CONVERSATION WITH EMILY

One day, Emily, one of my Taiwanese students, came into my office and blurted out:

"Because Sylvia's father is here, so do you want to see him?"

Puzzled, I queried, "Because?" and she nodded her head. "Do I want to meet him?" I asked, checking for understanding of her statements.

"Aha" she said nodding her head in agreement. "Because he does this [she motioned as if taking her pulse] and needles in your head. So do you want to see him?"

What was I to make of this? Inferences were quickly drawn (as Scollon and Scollon, 1995, pp. 10-11, point out about cross-cultural communication). I wasn't quite sure if I wanted to see someone I had never met, especially if it involved needles in my head, or some kind of hand or pulse checking.

Emily noticed my perplexity and explained, "He's a doctor, and does this [motioning again as if taking her pulse], and because Mr. Dewey already saw him and told him what all his problems, so do you want to see him next? Because he is leaving next Wednesday, then you can make another appointment for next week. . . ."

Thus proceeded a chunk of discourse, which at first puzzled me. Drawing from previous knowledge I inferred the following: 1) my other Taiwanese student's father must have come to visit from Taiwan 2) because I have a health problem, Emily thinks it would be a good idea for me to see this medical doctor 3) apparently, this doctor practices acupressure and/or acupuncture. My unspoken immediate response was only in my mind: NO! However, to make the conversation proceed happily, I said, "Yes, I would like to meet him sometime, but I am not sure if I want needles in my head."

"Don't be scared, it's OK," she shook her head. What had she inferred? Perhaps that I did want to make an appointment, not just meet somebody I did not know out of politeness.

The same apparent miscommunication may take place many times in the course of a teaching day, yet it is surprising how much real communication actually does take place anyway, in spite of cultural differences. What makes understanding of such discourse possible? There are more things that we as humans hold in common than things which make us different. How else would any communication take place across cultural, gender, generational, professional, social, and psychological boundaries? We all have to draw inferences about the code, the message, the meaning, the sounds, etc. We as interlocutors draw inferences and infer meanings from exchanges of discourse. Our thinking machine must process more than mere words, sounds, symbols, etc. Phonetics, phonology, morphology, syntax, semantics, pragmatics, psycholinguistics, sociolinguistics, non-verbal communication, schema—these are all parts of the communication puzzle. The exchange of a few words involves all of the above, and more. So how is it even possible for any communicative act to take place and for any of the interlocutors to actually communicate a message?

I believe there is a deep-rooted language and cognitive processor involved in the encoding and decoding of this communication system. It is a far more amazing computer than any man has yet invented! The capacity for language and thought far exceeds any other earthly endeavor, for upon this one—language alone—so many other endeavors hinge. Language is not our only cognitive capacity, but as humans we would be greatly hindered without this capacity. Perhaps that is why many religions of the world take the capacity for language as a miraculous God-given gift. What things we can accomplish with language!

By the way, I finally did get to meet Sylvia's father, and he did perform some rudimentary pulse feeling acupressure and told me I am too fat and need to lose weight! That is quite obvious, and no need of pulse feeling would have been necessary for such a splendid diagnosis and prognosis! So was the entire episode useless? Not really. It had served other non-linguistic purposes. I had actually met Sylvia's father; I had pleased my students; I had strengthened affective ties; I had actually met another member of the human family (who did not speak English) through my student's puzzling attempts at establishing a meeting. And all that because of miscommunication? I hardly think so! Many literacies had come together in this meeting of minds, languages, and cultures.

GOLDILOCKS AND THE TWO HAITIANS

As a professional communicator in an ESL classroom, I often must be aware that my students may or may not share the same world-knowledge (or cultural literacy) that I have. Also as a Christian minister, I am extremely aware that my literacy in this area is limited to certain social circles. Thus in communicating the Christian message to those unfamiliar with it, often times I must provide background knowledge before a meaningful discussion can take place.

Scollon and Scollon (1995) have said, "This sort of 'encyclopedic' knowledge of one's world is the sort that often causes confusion or miscommunication in intercultural communication," (p.58) and that is quite true! For example, when I was teaching about using analogy to develop paragraphs in a developmental English class, I had two Haitian students who had to be informed about a well-known fairy tale. I was giving an example of an analogy that I read one time: a friend was being compared to Goldilocks (in the Three Bears story) because this friend had the habit of coming into the house when the owner was away, of getting into the refrigerator for leftovers, of watching TV, of being found taking a nap on the sofa.

When I mentioned this analogy, I said, "You know the story of Goldilocks?"

My Haitian students answered, "No."

So, I had to retell the story of Goldilocks and the Three Bears to adult college students before they could understand the analogy and background knowledge; then, they wanted me to write the name of the story down for them so they could look it up later.

These students were genuinely interested in the use of that story for this particular analogy. So even though I was dealing with adult college students, they did not share this "encyclopedic" cultural literacy. If I had continued on with my explanation of analogy without stopping to ask whether they knew the story, much of my explanation would have gone over their heads!

THE CUBAN WOMAN AND THE PROPHETS

I carry around many literacies. For example, I preach and teach in Spanish as I work in a Spanish church setting as a Sunday School teacher for the adult class; I have people with different levels of knowledge of the Bible. One spring, as I taught the Minor Prophets, one Cuban elderly woman, an 83-year-old retired medical transcriber/translator, commented that she had not heard about the Minor Prophets since she was a little girl when her mother had commented on a verse from one of the prophets about the wrath of God. Though this woman had known the Bible stories and had some knowledge of the prophets, the actual lessons were new to her. I, a Mexican-American converted from Catholicism to Evangelicalism, was teaching in Spanish about the Hebrew Minor Prophets to a Cuban immigrant woman. Much background knowledge had to be provided for a correct understanding of the Minor Prophets in their own cultural context. Then doctrine could be derived and taught after mutual understanding between teacher and student. Thus it is evident that cultural knowledge is also involved in communication, and not just words! Such is cultural literacy.

PERFORMING THE KANJOBAL WEDDING

On one occasion I was asked if I could perform a wedding for a Kanjobal couple in one of the churches where I occasionally preach, in Lake Worth, Florida. Kanjobal is a Guatemalan Indian dialect of a modern tribe of the ancient Mayas. Many Kanjobal speakers attend this particular church. Spanish is a second language to many of them; in public school their children learn English as a second language, rather than Spanish.

I was astonished to see the bride march in! She was wearing a white blouse (just like a regular wedding gown top), but she was wearing her Kanjobal Indian, woven, multi-colored skirt! As I stood before the congregation performing the ceremony, I thought, "What am I doing here? Here I am a Mexican-American immigrant, converted from Catholicism to Evangelicalism, performing an American style Protestant wedding, for a Kanjobal Guatemalan Indian couple!" A true *meztisaje* taking place, not only of the new couple, but also of myself... After the wedding ceremony we enjoyed eating some Guatemalan style tamales made of rice flour and meat, rather than the traditional Mexican tamales with corn meal and meat.

What a delicious event! I savored every moment of the mixtures!

BACK TO THE IMPERFECT SEVEN

Perhaps this is a good place to return to my story about the imperfect seven.

While I was in college in South Texas, my linguistics teacher, from the eastern U. S., actually wrote her number seven on the board as a little cane crossed. At that time I felt delighted, appalled, and disappointed! Why was it that she could use the symbol for the number that had been stolen from me, and her students were not confusing it with an F? My linguistics teacher was highly educated. Why was it that other people I met later still used this symbol which I had been bereft of? In fact, I met others who even made the r ( ) as I knew it before, and they were not morons! What kind of literacy and numeracy was this? Actually I felt I had been cheated by a well-meaning fifth grade teacher in the U. S. who had tried to assimilate me into his own style of American culture. As a child, I had even been told that I was no longer supposed to speak Spanish anymore, but I was supposed to practice English only! A strange new world indeed! But, as it turned out, I have maintained my literacy in both languages, remaining bilingual and bicultural, comfortable even when I take graduate courses in English or graduate literature courses in Spanish, and reading/writing and interacting in graduate level English or Spanish!

And now I have come full circle. I know other linguistics professors and colleagues who also practice my form of numeracy; they write the number seven like my long lost little cane with a cross. I guess the baggage of literacy practices we go through as children sometimes in and of themselves can be like a cross to bear, even in old age when we use canes... así es la vida.

Chapter Nine

The View From Here

I started by relating some experiences in my life, both in Spanish and in English literacy, which speak to me of the bilingual/bicultural experience: a process of change, both culturally and linguistically. Now I want to reflect upon these as I try to find patterns, and I see three types of change: linguistic, cultural, and religious.

LINGUISTIC CHANGE

As often occurs with first generation children of immigrants, I became bilingual, speaking to my parents in Spanish, while using English to get along in the school community. Though my mother and father are somewhat bilingual, to this day, they have chosen to use Spanish in the home. This is a common pattern. Concerning a typical immigrant family and their language practices, Grosjean (1982) says:

> On arrival in the United States, the parents are generally monolingual in their native language (L1), and they may either remain monolingual or become bilingual in their native language and English (L2). To remain monolingual, that is, to use no English, the parents must live in a close-knit ethnic community where they can work, shop, converse with friends and relatives in their own language. This is [sic] often possible at the turn of the century in the areas where such groups as Franco-Americans and German Americans lived, and it is still possible today among Hispanics, Chinese, and Portuguese Americans, for instance. However, most first-generation Americans, especially if they are young, come into contact with the English-speaking majority and become bilingual. Most remain bilingual for the rest of their lives, but a few who have no way of maintaining their first language, who desire to assimilate quickly, or who actually

reject their native language (Russian Jews, for example) will become monolingual speakers of English. (pp. 103-104)

In contrast to many people such as Rodriguez (1982), I did not reject my valued first language; I love it and never have thought of it as inferior. Rodriguez says, "Education is a movement into another world," and there is "freedom to break out of a minority culture" (Victim, 1994), but my experience has differed from Rodriguez' so I feel I have not done what he did. While assimilation theory says one needs to learn to play the roles expected in order to succeed in the U S system, multiculturalism says one's multilingual skills are an asset to education and life skills (Lutz, 2004, p. 3). Lutz says that "segmented assimilation" posits that the shift to "English only" may actually result in "blocked social mobility and end in ghettoization" (p. 5).

When I became bilingual, I didn't break away from my first language, but I maintained it. My close ties to my parents in the Rio Grande Valley and family in Mexico have encouraged maintenance of my native language and culture. Many Anglo-Americans and other Hispanics may share Rodriguez' view of the need to break away from minority languages and cultures, perhaps because of the situation of the "conquered" Mexican people and territories, the political climate of "English only," and of course, the "dubious" political threat for the United States that the Spanish language appears to be in many people's eyes.

I believe I maintained my Spanish for several reasons. One of these was because of my close family, my continual use of Spanish with my parents, and our yearly trips to see relatives back in Mexico. I use my Spanish in church work on a regular basis, too. But more than that, I have always thought the bilingual person is worth two people, like my grandfather in Mexico had taught me.

As I mentioned earlier, it was in Chicago Heights that I felt the most change coming over me linguistically/ psychologically/culturally. I remember being asked questions in English by my sixth grade teacher that I was able to understand, and I myself was amazed at this ability. I thought it must have happened overnight! I believe the "silent" period of learning may have occurred in Corpus Christi, Texas. According to Grosjean (1982), "Public education is an important factor in language shift: minority children are taught in the majority language in an Anglo-American environment, and very quickly many of them begin to identify with the English language and its accompanying culture" (p. 110).

My siblings and I followed the pattern of the bilingual child, offspring of monolingual parents. My American-born brother, though bilingual, has married a Mexican-born immigrant, and speaks Spanish at home; my other Mexican-born brother has also married a Tex-Mex bilingual woman and his home is bilingual. Meanwhile I married Cynthia, my sweetheart for years, an Anglo-American, bilingual in English/Spanish. In my home, we are basically English speakers, but my wife's graduate studies in Spanish literature and our church ministries keep us using Spanish. My children are encouraged to become bilingual, though they are definitely dominant in English. When my oldest boy was seventeen, I asked him, "Andrew, do you think your bilingual abilities are an asset?" He answered, "Definitely!" When I asked John-Mark, my youngest son (who was then sixteen), he answered, "What bilingual abilities?" He, of course, considers himself more dominant in English and weaker in Spanish. Nonetheless, both of them took Spanish in high school and Spanish for bilinguals in college. They both went on to take third year college Spanish, and function fairly well in the language. Though it did take an effort on our part as parents, they have been bilingual throughout their young lives. Along these lines, Zentella (1998) argues there is a "poisonous stereotype" in which "[m]any U. S. Americans believe that the very fabric of the nation's life is being torn apart as we approach the twenty-first century, and some blame those who speak another language and attempt to raise their children bilingually" (p. 11). Tom Barry (2005) argues further:

> Anti-immigrant movements are, of course, nothing new in the United States. Campaigns against new immigrants have generally coincided with the business cycle, rising in intensity with economic slowdowns, declining in times of prosperity. There are two main corollaries to this rule. One, the US public generally views immigrants with more or less hostility according to the color of their skin, their English-speaking abilities, and the degree to which their religion and culture depart from Judeo-christianity. . . . [I]n times of war, immigrants from nations in conflict with the United States are especially suspect. (p. 1)

My boys feel themselves quite American, not so much Mexican. Yet my family and I appear as part of that "threat" to U. S. culture, I suppose, since we are bilingual and encourage everybody else to be bilingual, no matter what two languages!

The 2006 controversy in the US Senate over declaring English the national language has fueled the debate even more. However, research by Lutz (2004) reports positive results for bilingualism and bicultural abilities:

> High school completion was highest for biliterate students (86.1%) and English monolinguals (85%) . . . students. Enrollment in a college program was also highest for biliterate (41%) and English-dominant (40%) students, followed closely by oral bilingual students (39%), and then by English monolinguals (33%). Biliterates had higher levels of enrollment in a bachelor's degree programs [sic]—about one-quarter were enrolled—compared to slightly less than one-fifth of the students from the other high-English-proficiency groups. (p. 6)

I am part of the 1.5 generation, a child of immigrant parents, educated and growing up in the US. I have obtained by Ph.D. in English, but I also have graduate level course work in Spanish, and am considering obtaining another Ph.D. in Hispanic Linguistics. When I got married, my own home became basically Americanized. My marriage to an Anglo-American English speaker, who became bilingual in Spanish, has contributed to my Americanization more strongly. Yet since my wife and I were missionaries in Mexico for a couple of years and later settled for a while in the Tex-Mex culture of the Rio Grande Valley, I have grown to accept these cultural tensions. Having lived in Mexico for two years as an adult, I realized there that I was not really a Mexican purely—I was a foreigner. Like Ulla connor (1999, p. 36), I underwent a metamorphosis.

CULTURAL CHANGE

In the Rio Grande Valley, while studying for my MA in ESL, I finally decided to become an American citizen. My conscious decision to become American was a definite emotional struggle for identity and political loyalty. I realized I was going to become one of the labeled minorities in the U. S., a hyphenated Mexican-American; I had to give up my allegiance to my beloved country, but I guess I had actually lost my allegiance years before. Keefe and Padilla (1987) claim that "cultural change is an orderly process that occurs between immigrants and their later generational offspring" (pp. 52-53). In my case, I had a lot of anomie; I did not necessarily go through this "orderly process," but it was *definitely a process of change*.

My boys are basically Americanized, being enculturated in American style schooling in the U.S. They have maintained a high degree of American culture, though both appreciate the Mexican culture, especially the Tex-Mex culture, since in their growing up years we lived with them in the Rio Grande Valley. They both enjoy Mexican food — *tacos, tamales, chiles rellenos* — but especially hot stuff like *salsa* and *chile*; they both love visiting relatives in Mexico; they both practice their Spanish every opportunity they get. In fact, both have traveled to Spanish speaking countries to do short term summer missions work, including Guatemala and Mexico. In the summer of 2005, my son Andrew was doing short term missions working with the youth in Ciudad Victoria, Mexico, while my other son John-Mark was taking a couple of civil engineering classes at the Tecnológico in Monterey, Mexico.

Nonetheless, my sons are definitely American first, Mexican-American second.

RELIGIOUS CHANGE

Another pattern is the religious change, though not always acknowledged in academics. Not all, but many immigrants also have switched religious affiliations throughout history. Many of those Mexicans who have switched turned to evangelical, Pentecostal, Baptist, or independent churches. In the early 1900s "Americanization for [many] also meant Protestantization," from Catholic into mainline churches (Rolle, 1968, p. 303). My family's pattern is not uncommon. There is however, social stigma and ostracism which was (and still is) common when people change religious beliefs. Historically, many native born Americans have tended to stigmatize Catholics, while those Catholics who converted, going outside Catholicism, were ostracized by the Catholics. This double marginalization was especially difficult. However, new converts found that a church family provided the moral support needed for social adjustment. Smith (1978), writing about the early 1900s immigrants, argues that "migration was often a theologizing experience" (p. 1175). He continues:

> The individual's sense of responsibility for the decision to migrate was primarily here. Loneliness, the romanticizing of memories, the guilt for imagined desertion of parents and other relatives, and the search for community and identity in a world of strangers all began the moment the nearest range of hills shut out the view of the emigrant's native valley. Longing for a past that could not be recovered intensified the emotional satisfaction of daring to hope for a better future. Separation from both personal and physical associations of one's childhood community drew emotional strings taut. Friendships, however, were often fleeting; and the lonely vigils—when sickness, unemployment, or personal rejection set individuals apart—produced deep crises of the spirit. At such moments, concrete symbols of order or hope that the village church and priest and the annual round of religious observances had once provided seemed far away; yet the mysteries of individual existence as well as the confusing agonies of anomie cried out for religious explanation . . . . (p. 1174)

This sense of anomie is a very tender spot for cultural, linguistic, and religious change. Speaking about the 1900s immigrants, Smith declares "Notions of pilgrimage and expectations of personal and cultural change magnified concern for a basis of moral and religious authority that could provide a sense of permanence to those adapting themselves to shifting social realities" (Smith, 1978, 1179). Furthermore, he continues, "Belief and devotion were powerful impulses to accommodation and innovation; both helped legitimate the behavior, the perceptions, and the structures of association that sustained the processes of change" (Smith, 1978, p. 1181). Though my parents immigrated to the US in 1968, in my case, this religious change appears to follow the same pattern as the immigrants in the early 1900s. In fact, in the church work my wife and I do, we have found that it is easier for a newly arrived immigrant to convert to evangelicalism, than for an immigrant who has already assimilated into the American cultural system and patterns. I don't know why this is the case, but I think it is like the case of the immigrants in the 1900s.

Rodriguez (1982), though not necessarily changing religious affiliations, has also undergone a religious change as he claims in his autobiography. In the chapter entitled "Credo," he confessed that he once longed for a past ceremonial ritual church, though he is basically a liberal Catholic now. He laments the new liturgy in the vernacular English and longs for the Old Latin Mass. However, he does assert: "I will continue to go to the English mass. I will go because it is my liturgy. I will, however, often recall with nostalgia the faith I have lost. And I will be uneasy knowing that the old faith was lost as much by *choice* [sic] as it was inevitably lost" (pp. 114-5). Thus Rodriguez, by his own admission, is a Catholic by tradition, not by true old-fashioned Catholicism, in the strictest sense: "By choice I do not consult the movie ratings of the Legion of Decency, and my reading is not curtailed by the Index. By choice I am ruled by conscience rather than the authority of priests I consider my equals. I do not listen to papal pronouncements with which I disagree" (p. 115). He thus professes his own brand of "Catholicism," antagonistically different from what he communally professed in his youthful days as an acolyte in the church. This change came about in Rodriguez' life during his college education. When he read about "Protestant" Christians, Rodriguez says he could identify more with their belief systems: "It was then that I began to realize the difference separating the individualistic Protestant from the institutional Catholic. Now I realize that I have become like a Protestant Christian. I call myself a Christian" (p. 117).

PATTERNS IN PROGRESS

Thus, a pattern seems to emerge from my life: I am a first generation Mexican-American, undergoing linguistic, cultural, and religious change. I was only ten when my parents decided to immigrate to the United States, my age perhaps facilitating my linguistic and cultural change - - the acculturation and adaptation, if you will. English has become my dominant language, though perhaps I would classify my language learning experience as sequential bilingualism. American culture has shaped my way of being. In fact, when I returned to live in Mexico for a few years in my adult life, I found I could not fit in very well; I was an American, as much a foreigner as any other foreigner. I was even converted from Catholicism to Protestantism, my relatives in Mexico criticizing our "betrayal."

Again, as I stated at the beginning, I must finish by making clear that I am an American; my political loyalty is to my beloved adopted country, The United States of America. This book entails the process of my change from a Mexican child of immigrant parents to an adult American citizen. It's a

Figure 9.1. Eagle, serpent, and flag

process that has involved cultural, linguistic, and (for me, at least) also religious change. At this stage, I believe I have learned to live with the process of change and acculturation. With this book I hope people can see that generation 1.5 children of immigrant parents do not have to fail as some researchers of generation 1.5 people seem to imply. Rather, we can succeed in the process of language and culture learning. We generation 1.5 children of immigrant parents can benefit from learning English, adopting American culture, and being politically loyal to our adopted country. At the same time, we can maintain our cultural ties with our former roots and even maintain our mother tongue as an asset to our lives and a cultural asset in our new adopted country, the United States of America. As my grandfather used to say, the bilingual person is worth two! Immigration for any person means change, inevitable change. But change can be a process of discovery and challenge, if the immigrant learns to adjust, accept, and hope.

Appendix

Immigrant Children at Ellis' Door

While I was studying for my Ph.D. in English in 1998, specializing in rhetoric and linguistics, I did some naturalistic inquiry doing some biographical work of a senior citizen (now deceased) who had been a child of Italian immigrant parents in the 1900s. His story is typical of immigrants and children of immigrants in the 1900s; based on his life, I wrote a long unpublished poem during my graduate studies, a poem which I'd like to append to my book. I believe it parallels my story in some ways, and the story of many other immigrants. Arturo's (fictitious name) story involved linguistic, cultural, and religious changes, just like my story. His father was from Parma, Italy, immigrating to the US in the early 1900s, and he underwent a surname change, as did many immigrants in that time period. His family lived in the coal mine camps in Pennsylvania, where immigrants from various European countries worked. In the process of change, Arturo lost his Italian language, learned English as his dominant language, and early in his life became converted from Catholicism to Evangelicalism. Some of the family's "vices" Arturo related included wine drinking and gambling. When he was a child, the children would gamble matches (which he would steal from his mother's kitchen) for lack of money, during the depression years. He called this gambling "Matchy Poker." Arturo's grandparents were furious when they learned that Arturo's family had become converted and ostracized them. Upon his dad's conversion, his dad became involved in the slashing of wine barrels, a practice popular in the prohibition era. After Arturo went to college and served in the army, he married a preacher's daughter and his family became very American. I met and interviewed him when he was a senior citizen who loved working on his vegetable garden. Based on his life's story, I created the following poem, *Immigrant Children at Ellis' Door*. It typifies the lives of early immigrants to the United States, especially the lives of the children of immigrants.

Immigrant's Children at Ellis' Door

Leaving Parma, was my Dad
    barely twenty, sailed ahead
        to America then he came
Quickly had to change his name.

Nineteen nineteen, I was born
    America, my new home
        coal mine camping, ain't no fun
Immigrant's children overrun.

In the coal mines, had to work
    in America, ain't no sport
        Filthy, dirty, clothed in soot
Coal mine camping pays low loot.

Italiano parlo io,
    in mia casa, not no mo'
        not no grammar, Dad does know
Though my Momma, third grade go.

Russia, Hungary, Italy, too
    in the coal camp, immigrant stew
        teacher only, English knew
Melting pot's got a new brew.

Now I know my ABC,
    won't you come and sing with me
        English only, then we spoke
For the teacher, it's no joke!

"Matchy" poker, Mom didn't know
    why her matches were all stole
        and at thirteen, who will win?
Coal mine camping, life of sin.

Forehead crossing, went to bed
    coal mine camping, life was dead
        drinking, swearing, poker play
Problems I had with my way.

Prohibition came by lead,
    nineteen thirties just ahead
        at the tent house, people rouse

"Be free from sin" so we got in.
Amazing Grace, how sweet the sound
        into the fold, I'm coming round
                change religion, round the bend
Catholic friends, couldn't understand.

My friends called us, holly rollers
    called me bishop, and more slop
        preacher, bishop, honkey-lot
Stigmatized, within, without.

Italiano parlo io
    in mia casa, not no mo'
        not no grammar, Dad does know
Though my Momma, third grade go.

Oldest girl, my Momma was,
    wrote to Grandma- - quite a loss
        Grandma came right into town
But didn't want us hanging round.

Devastated Momma was
    "Not my daughter you will be,
        Grandma's coming you won't see"
Lord will help you, long to live.

Valentino was my Dad,
    of conversion, he was MAD
        now Italians, made their wine
Just for friendship, that was fine.

When I was sick, Mom did make
    boiled wine for me to take
        but as I said, Dad was MAD
Going to church for him was bad!

"As for me, can give up wine,
    what shall I do, when friends come?"
        and those days, to church we went
While my Dad, to wrath gave vent.

So things kept a heating up
    Mom in Jesus growing up
        Papa's brother made more fun
"Can't you keep that woman down?"

"Give me money," then he said
    as the children, went to bed
        "If you don't stop going to church,"
"I will leave you in the lurch!"

Crying Momma said to me, "Keep the children,
    Not to suffer, there's no need"
        I said, "Momma, please don't go"
But she went to church once mo'.

Dad was raging, pacing floor
    as I thought, see him no more
        though he raved, he did not go,
'Twas a turning point, I know.

Mom inviting, "Go with me."
    Daddy fumming, "Let me be!"
        "Going to that church, ain't my goal,
'Til your preacher, helps load coal!"

Then one day, "I go," he say
    Mom prayed that he'd find the Way.
        and that Sunday, he got saved
After that, no more he raved.

He slashed barrels, the next day
    liquid slam and barrel slay
        "Give them to me," neighbors pled
"Ain't good for you or me!" he said.

Leaving Parma, was my Dad
    barely twenty, sailed ahead
        to America then he came
Quickly had to change his name.

Filthy, dirty, clothed in soot
    coal mine camping, pays low loot
        went to college, I made friends
Stepped outside, my Italian ends.

After army, married wife,
    and together made a life
        preacher's daughter married me
and my parents, said, "Glory!"

Immigrant Children at Ellis' Door

Italiano parlo io,
    in mia casa, not no mo'
        not no grammar, Dad does know
Though my mama, third grade go.

Now the melting pot's no goal
    'stead we call it, salad bowl
        come from Parma, Mexico
Hungary, Russia at Ellis' door.

Ellis statue's open door
    clamors loudly, "Give me More!"
        Immigrant's children, salad make
Culture, language, away we take!

Plant tomatoes, garlic too
    onion pepper, salad's good
        but for salad bowl we'll take
Immigrant's children, a new make.

Works Consulted and Cited

Anzaldúa, G. (1987). *Borderlands: la frontera.* San Francisco: Aunt Lute Books.

Barry, T. (2005, May-June). Anti-immigrant backlash on the "home front.": (Report: The War on Terror). *NACLA Report on the Americas.* Retrieved June 8, 2006, from http://.searchflelibrary.org:80/v/EG64B9BT8MLD8P63J65N3U7HJ1 GH228SYB1GSKL7AK5LLT7F8P-44453?func+find-db-6-next&set-entry= 000011.

Baynham, M. (1995). *Literacy practices: investigating literacy in social contexts.* London: Longman Group.

Connor, U. (1999). Learning to write academic prose. In G. Braine, (ed.) *Non-native educators in English language teaching.* (pp. 29-42), Mahweh, N. J.: Lawrence Erlbaum Associates.

Ferdman, B. M. (1990, May). Literacy and cultural identity. *Harvard Educational Review* 60(2), 181-204.

Freire, P. (1988). The adult literacy process as cultural action for freedom and education and conscientizacao. In E. R. Kingten, B. M. Kroll, & M. Rose (Eds.). *Perspectives on Literacy.* (pp. 398-409). Carbondale: Southern Illinois University.

Gee, J. P. (1991). What is literacy? In C. Mirchell & K. Weiler (Eds.), *Rewriting literacy: culture and the discourse of the other* (pp. 3-11). Connecticut: Bergin & Garvey.

Grosjean, F. (1982). *Life with two languages.* Cambridge: Harvard U. Press.

Kaplan, A. (1993). *French Lessons: a memoir.* Chicago: Univ. of Chicago Press.

Keefe, S. E. and A. Padilla (1987). *Chicano ethnicity.* Albuquerque, New Mexico: U. Of New Mexico Press.

Lutz, A. (2004, July-Dec.). Dual language proficiency and the educational attainment of Latinos. *Migraciones Internacionales.* (2:4) p. 95 (28). Retrieved June 8, 2006 from http:/search.flelibrary.org:80/V/EG64B9BT8MLD8P63J65N347HJ1GH22 ...&short-format=002&set_number=0008834&set-entry=000021&format=999.

Mitchell, C and K. Weiler (1991). *Rewriting literacy: culture and the discourse of the other.* Wesport, Connecticut: Bergin & Garvey.

Padgett, R. (1995). *Creative reading: what it is, how to do it, and why.* Urbana, Ill.: National Council of Teachers of English.

Palacios, I. (2001). *An ESL/literacy center: A qualitative study of perspectives and practices of immigrant adults and literacy facilitators.* Unpublished doctoral dissertation, Indiana University of Pennsylvania, Indiana, PA.

Ramsdell, L. (2004, Fall). Language and identity politics: the linguistic autobiographies of Latinos in the United States. *Journal of Modern Literature* (28:1), p. 166 (11). Retrieved 8 June, 2006 from http://search.flelibrary.org:80/VEG64B9BT8 MLD8P63J65N3U7HJ1GH22...&short-format=002&set-number=000878&set-entry=000002&format=999.

Rodriguez, R. (1982). *Hunger of memory: the education of Richard Rodriguez.* New York: Dial Press/ Random House.

Rolle, A. F. (1968). *The immigrant upraised.* Norman, Oklahoma: U. of Oklahoma Press.

Rosenbaum, R. (1981). *Mexicano resistance in the Southwest: the sacred right of self preservation.* Austin: U of Texas Press.

Scollon, R. and S. W. Scollon (1995). *Intercultural communication.* Malden, Mass.: Blackwell.

Smith, F. (1988). *Joining the literacy club: further essays into education.* Portsmouth, New Hampshire: Heineman.

Smith, T. L. (1978, Dec.). Religion and ethnicity in America. *American Historical Review.* (83:5), 1155-1185

Street, B (1984). *Literacy in theory and practice.* Cambridge, England: Cambridge U. P.

Victim of two cultures: Richard Rodriguez (1994). [Videotape]. Princeton, N. J.: Films for the Humanities.

Zentella, A. C. (1997). *Growing up bilingual.* Malden, Mass.: Blackwell Publishers.

About the Author

Until he was ten years old, **Dr. Ignacio Palacios** grew up in Monterrey, Mexico, so Spanish is his first language. However, his family's immigration to the United States in the late 1960s has made of him an American, with English as his dominant second language. He has his Ph.D. in English, with a concentration in Rhetoric and Linguistics from Indiana University of Pennsylvania (2001) and an MA in English as a Second Language from the University of Texas-Pan American (1988). Dr. Palacios teaches TESOL courses, linguistics related courses, literature and composition courses, and Spanish courses. He lives with his wife, Cynthia, in Texas. In addition to their academic work, they are both involved in Spanish church work. In his spare time, Dr. Palacios enjoys reading and travel; as a hobby, he likes creating and collecting marionettes, creating and collecting nativity scenes (*nacimientos*) and making piñatas, as well as having piñata parties!

www.ingramcontent.com/pod-product-compliance
Lightning Source LLC
Chambersburg PA
CBHW020126240426

43673CB00038B/615